EDUCATION EMERGENCY

Closing the Achievement Gap for At-Risk and
Minority Youth in Urban Schools.

West Shaw

Printed in the United States of America

ISBN- 13: 978-1-7333969-3-6

10 9 8 7 6 5 4 3 2 1

EMPIRE PUBLISHING

www.empirebookpublishing.com

"It is easier to build strong children than to repair broken men." – *Frederick Douglas*

Dedication

I am dedicating this work to the past, present, and the future:

To the past - my amazing former students and colleagues who have helped me to become a better teacher.

To the present - my current students and coworkers who challenge me and teach me new things every day.

To the future - the future students that I am excited to one day meet, educate, motivate, and inspire.

Preface

I write this book with a deep belief, that all students of color, including those that may be growing up in urban, disadvantaged, high needs, economically distressed and or violent neighborhoods have the ability to overcome these obstacles and reach academic and career success despite the overwhelming odds, trauma and adversity they may face. I believe that teachers and schools are in the position and have the unique ability to powerfully impact and transform the lives of students and their families. I have developed this unshakable belief because I truly believe roses can indeed grow from cracks in the concrete, and I know that we too, can grow and thrive under the most adverse conditions.

There are some resilient students that manage to flourish despite their backgrounds, addresses or zip codes. There are students that thrive despite attending schools located in emergency areas of need. I have witnessed students excel despite the overwhelming obstacles positioned in front of them. I know that our urban and minority youth can succeed academically. I believe it can be done. I have seen it done, and I know it is being done, in my classroom and in a growing number of dynamic and innovative classrooms around the country every day.

This book, Education Emergency is necessary because urban education is in a state of crisis. The endless cycle of teachers abandoning our urban youth and fleeing inner-city schools for their suburban counterparts, out of classroom positions or other professions has been and continues to be a tremendous problem. Teachers are walking away from the profession in droves due to the frustration and stress that comes with the job. Additionally, over the past decade, the sky-rocketing price of college tuition and the student loan debt crisis have left students trying to figure out if they can even afford to go to college or how they will pay back student loan debt upon graduation. We have truly reached a state of emergency when our most vulnerable students began to question if going to college is even worth it. Furthermore, the steadily increasing price of rent in urban areas in combination with the lack of opportunity to land mid to high wage jobs is creating a serious quality of life problem for our urban youth. Compounding this problem is the issue that students living and attending schools in economically distressed and or high crime communities are being exposed to an excessive amount of violence. Students from disadvantaged, urban, areas are constantly exposed to economic, physical, cultural, social, spiritual and mental trauma. This book provides remedies and recommendations for urban teachers to help at-risk youth succeed in the classroom and overcome challenges they may face growing up and attending schools in these stressful and violent communities.

There are a countless number of books addressing topics such as poverty, violence, minority and urban education. Half of these books look at these issues from a historical context and do not provide any real useful strategies for today's urban teacher. The other half of these books provide strategies that are highly unlikely to work in a real-world urban classroom located in an emergency area of need. This book is important and unique because it does both. Not only will this book discuss the forces and issues that shape urban education, but it will also provide remedies and strategies for teaching in today's urban schools.

Forward

When I began my teaching experience at an urban, high-needs middle school back in 2004, I did not know what to expect. I had taken classes and workshops about lesson planning, classroom management, assessment, differentiation, and the like, but there was much about the day-to-day experience that these classes and workshops failed to adequately address: How do I effectively reach the students in my specific context, many of whom are performing well below grade level and face a variety of challenges with which I cannot personally identify? What actually works?

Shaw's book, Education Emergency, aims to bridge that gap. Drawing from more than fifteen years of experience teaching in urban settings, West offers tips for meeting the physical, social, emotional, and spiritual demands of students in high-needs schools. While there are many challenges that students and teachers in high-needs schools face (both on an individual and systemic level), this book focuses on what is within the teacher's locus of control, i.e., the classroom setting.

The work of creating truly equitable classroom environments for all students is not easy. It requires wisdom, discernment, caring, patience, reflection, and time. Shaw's book offers a helpful guide along this journey, providing encouragement and support to teachers who are doing this important work in high-needs settings.

Tolulope Noah, EdD
Assistant Professor of Liberal Studies
Azusa Pacific University

Warning!

I did not write this book for critics or skeptics. I wrote this book for people who want to make a difference in education. I wrote this book for educators who want to create positive change in their students, classrooms, schools, and communities. I wrote this book to motivate, encourage and inspire teachers working in our urban schools. I wrote this book to help improve the overall quality of urban education.

That said, my teaching practice and message have been heavily influenced by the Adverse Childhood Experience Study (ACEs) 1998. The results of the ACEs study generally suggest that adverse childhood experiences have a substantially negative impact on a person's future health, social, economic, and lifelong learning opportunities. Some examples of adverse childhood experiences may include physical abuse, emotional abuse, sexual abuse, post-traumatic stress disorder, parental mental illness, emotional or physical neglect and extreme poverty. Research from this study explained that, over time, the development of children's brains may actually be negatively altered due to continuous exposure to traumatic experiences and that these changes could make it increasingly difficult to learn or become academically successful. The Aces findings seemed to indicate that students who have been exposed to several adverse situations are far more likely to experience academic, behavioral, health, and truancy issues. The various negative consequences associated with adverse childhood experiences supports the need to significantly reduce students' exposure to these negative experiences. The prevailing recommendation from those who have reviewed the ACEs study, is to create safe, stable, nurturing relationships, and environments for all children and that's exactly what Education Emergency aims to help you do. This book is going to help you transform your urban classroom into an engaging, nurturing and supportive environment where all kids can thrive and feel safe enough to learn and achieve academic success.

How to Get Most out of This Book

- Have an open mind. Allow yourself to consider new ideas, methods, and possibilities.

- Take notes. Jot down key points for reflection.

- Read with a purpose. Consider two or three things you would like to accomplish after reading this text.

- Create next steps. While reading, develop one or two next steps that you will attempt in your classroom.

- Reflect on your practice. Pause after each chapter and reflect on your own practice.

- Have discussion. Answer discussion questions and start conversations about topics covered in this book.

- Put ideas into action. Working with your professional learning community (PLC) create a plan of action and begin implementing your favorite principles in your school or classroom.

- Share it. Share this book with your colleagues, coworkers, classmates and friends on social media and help drive deeper conversations and spread the word about emergency teaching.

Teacher's Hippocratic Oath

I vow to fulfill to the best of my ability this promise.

I will respect and acknowledge the hard-won scientific gains of those educators in whose steps I walk and will gladly share any valuable knowledge acquired with those who are to follow after me.

I will apply for the benefit of every student all measures that are required, avoiding those twin traps of over assessment, and teaching to the test.

I will remember that teaching is an art as well as a science and that warmth, sympathy, and understanding may outweigh the administrator's goals or teacher's lesson plan.

I will not be ashamed to say "I DON'T KNOW" or seek help from a colleague when I am feeling stressed, frustrated, overwhelmed or uncertain.

I will respect the privacy of my students for their needs were entrusted to me not to be shared with the world. Most especially must I tread with care in matters of abuse and neglect. If it is given me to save a life, all thanks. But it may also be within my power to fail to act; this awesome responsibility must be faced with great humbleness and awareness of my own frailty. Above all, I must remember that I am here to serve.

I will remember that I do not teach a deficit, test score or an IEP, but a growing human being, whose needs may affect the person's family and economic stability. My responsibility includes these related problems, if I am to care adequately for my students.

I will teach prevention whenever I can, for prevention is preferable to cure.

I will remember that I remain a member of society, with special obligations to all my fellow human beings, those sound of mind and body as well as the infirm.

If I fulfill this oath, may I enjoy life and art, be respected while I live and remembered by my students with affection thereafter. May I always act so as to preserve the finest traditions of my calling and may I long experience the joy of healing those who seek my help.

Inspired by Louis Lasagna – 1964 Tufts University

Chapter One

Safe Enough to Learn?

It is 7:32 a.m. on a Monday, as I pull off the 105 Freeway and turn right on to Imperial Highway and then make a quick left onto Compton Ave. I'm rolling through South-Central Los Angeles, headed into the heart of the Watts neighborhood to teach another day of sixth-grade math and science. I pull over to grab my daily morning breakfast burrito from my favorite taco truck. Smoke fills the air, with the smell of breakfast being cooked by dozens of food trucks parked up and down the street. I pour green salsa over my burrito as I notice hundreds of students walking to school. Most are coming out of one of the notorious local housing projects: Nickerson Gardens, Jordan Downs, or Imperial Courts.

I head toward the school in my car, the light is green, but I and many other vehicles are at a complete stop. I am waiting patiently for students who slowly drag across the intersection while they proudly display their gang colors. Red baseball caps and red shoelaces clutter the intersection as they ignore the crossing guard's plea to hurry. Students walk around, step over, and seemingly ignore the dozens of homeless people sleeping, begging for change or pushing grocery baskets up and down the street. Students take the long route to school to avoid any interaction with the gang unit, which is a specialized police task force assigned to the area. I assume they are checking young men loitering outside an unopen laundry mat for drugs, weapons, and gang affiliations. Students flood out from the corner liquor store carrying their lunches, which consist of bags of potato chips, sunflower seeds, candy, and bottles of soda. Boys point and whistle at the women pacing the street corners wearing incredibly short skirts and high heels, pausing only long enough to gauge the genuine interest of any potential customer slowly rolling by. A small group of students huddle around at the bus stop and finish their morning smoking session before school begins. Some of these same students routinely attempt to bring marijuana and prescription pills on campus to make a little extra money for their families or themselves. Several groups of students walk the wrong way, heading away from the school, walking back toward their homes opting to skip school for the day instead of going to class. A few girls pause their morning procession to school to practice their dance moves on the church steps. The girls use their phones to make videos for social media. The young ladies listening to the newest exotic dancer turned music artist, seem to twerk twice as hard when they notice any boys walking nearby. Another group of female students walk to school in complete bliss, focused entirely on whatever boy has them wrapped up in their arms for that day. Two separate groups of boys play basketball and soccer at the park across the street from the school, often refusing to stop and come to class, until the final point is scored.

Alone and in large groups, students slowly wander through an urban jungle with rundown houses and stolen or abandoned cars. Students appear to be apathetic and unexcited about the day ahead as they make their journey to school passing over railroad tracks, through trash-filled alleyways, graffiti-covered walls and candle-lit memorials. A few students head to school in dirty and tattered clothing, some often wearing the same uniform shirt they wore the previous day. Many students might come to school without having had the opportunity to take a warm shower that morning or the previous night before. Students head to school with no backpack, no homework, no supplies, no enthusiasm, and seemingly no expectations for the day of learning ahead. Students walk to school in fear through a community of hopelessness, dragging invisible chains of anger, bound by poverty, shackled to systematic oppression. I often think about these students and wonder about their plans, dreams and goals for the future.

12

I watch nervously, as students jump out of moving cars in the middle of the street and dodge traffic as their parents rush off to work. I wait behind a car in the school parking lot blasting the explicit version of the latest hot rap song. It's a terrible song, but, it's so catchy and has a great beat. I can't help but to sing along.

A student gets out of the car wearing a purple hat, purple belt, purple backpack, three hundred-dollar purple sneakers and jokingly throws up a gang sign to his boys waiting out front. The boys basically lose their minds when they see his new limited - edition suede kicks and they spontaneously bust out in celebration dancing around the boy and throwing up their hoods. Near the side entrance a large group of kids form a circle around their fellow students as those in the middle participate in some epic rap battles. I am amazed at how talented and gifted some of these students are. We have some amazing lyricist, athletes, singers and dancers at our school and in this community. I ask myself time and time again, why are kids that are so amazingly talented continuing to struggle academically in the classroom? What are we doing wrong? Where is the disconnect? What do we need to do differently? The students spill into the entrance of the school which looks eerily similar to a prison with guards, dogs, metal detectors, large cement walls, and tall chain link gates topped with razor wire. I pull into a parking spot, turn off the ignition, grab my backpack and give myself the usual pep talk; "I am not going to get fired today." I say a quick prayer before walking toward the office to sign in for the day. "Heavenly Father, please help me to be kind and patient today, and help me to make a difference - Amen." In the hallway, on my way to class, I walk past a first-year teacher and yell out, "Only 145 more days to go!" "Just kill me now," she replies. I turn the corner and see the vice principal arguing with a substitute teacher. "I'm sorry," she says, with tears in her eyes. "I can't do this anymore. I don't know what I'm doing in the classroom. I feel like it's out of control" The vice principal tries to reason with the young lady. I realize we are about to lose another teacher. **Another one bites the dust.**

Walking through the campus, I see what I usually see: Students huddle in racially segregate groups. Graffiti covers the lockers, walls, and desks. The shabby grounds are covered in trash. Teachers walk to their classes looking tired and overwhelmed. The students, still in no hurry, walk into the classrooms late, unprepared, and give every indication that they are uninterested, unmotivated and unwilling to work hard.

I often observe students in other classes, and they seem resistant to learning. The students look bored and restless. Frequently the students are rude and disrespectful to each other as well as their teachers. My observations lead me to believe that the students are capable but afraid to try and seemingly unafraid to fail. Sometimes, I wonder if students worry about looking too smart in front of their peers. I believe that many of the struggling students are capable of academic achievement if they desired to do so. But instead, they make a conscious decision to shut down at school to show their resistance to what they may perceive to be a system of authority and oppression.

At lunchtime, I watch students from my classroom window kick on classroom doors and run down the hall, playing a never-ending game of hide-and-seek with the school security crew. Outside my window, I listen to a group of girls gossip about a former friend whom they now describe as just some "Dirty, dumb, broke, ugly slut." I hear another group, just outside my door, talking about how ugly, stupid, and poor, each other's mamas are. I watch in frustration as what seems like hundreds of students walk by gazing at either a phone, tablet, or smartwatch even though the campus has a no-electronic-devices policy. The students spend a disturbing amount of time staring at their phones and checking their social media and taking selfies throughout the school day. I gaze at the graffiti on the brick wall across from my room. It reads "MS-13 GANG MI CORDAZON, Mi VIDA, MI FAMILIA."

Three fights broke out on campus before lunch today. I get an email from the Principal, "A gang shooting and a retaliation shooting in the projects over the weekend have added to the constant tension on campus. Please stand out on supervision and help out this week." Ten minutes into lunch and the number of fights has doubled for the day. Students gather in uncomfortable numbers. Lunch period ends early, and as an effort to keep the campus safe, the school goes on lockdown. An email from the principal explains, there should not be any movement on campus by any students unless escorted by an adult.

My fifth-period students run to my class, overly excited about the events that took place during lunch. One student, Briana comes storming through the door, slamming her backpack down on the desk saying, "I'm tired of these big, stupid, ugly looking people always in my business, somebody bout to get hurt." At that exact moment, Cornelius runs through the other door, yelling, "Oh My God! Grape street! Purple rags! Grape street! Bounty Hunter Killer! Mr. Shaw, you should have seen it, they was tryna jump us! It's gonna be poppin' after school!" Cornelius breaks into a pop-locking dance routine to indicate how "poppin" it's about to be afterschool. As if almost on cue, the twins, Jessica and Leslie, come running through the door. First, the twins join the dance party with Cornelius. "Hey!, Heyyyy!!, Heyyyy!!!", Leslie says, as she hits the Whip and the Nae-Nae dance, encouraging Cornelius to keep getting it, on the improvised dance floor. Jessica yells, "Oh my God, did y'all see Melvin get beat up? I think he's dead," she jokes, "It was so funny!" Cornelius turns toward Nyla, "Nyla you better run home today, they gonna get you too." Nyla replies, "I ain't running nowhere." She said with confidence to Cornelious. "If somebody touches me, my brothers and cousins will come up here and exterminate these roaches." Cornelius and Nyla turn their attention to Briana. "Briana was about to get beat up"

Cornelius laughs and points. Briana explodes, "Yea right! Shut up! Ain't nobody ever beat me up, and that's on my mama." Briana continues, "Latino pride over here! I will see anybody at this school. I'm not afraid of nobody! My momma told me, don't let nobody punk me or talk mess about me." Cornelius replies, "Latino pride? No thanks! Take that crap back to Mexico." Briana explodes, "I'm not from Mexico, I'm from the projects. Now, don't you feel stupid!" The class erupts in laughter. Finally, I had enough, I interrupt, "Okay, okay, kids relax, we know you can fight Briana, but can you divide fractions? Because that's all I care about today, let's beat some math problems up, and get to work." Nyla interrupts, "Awwwwe, Mr. Shaw, why you always making us work?" I reply, "Because I care." The class erupts in laughter again. Cornelius replies, "Yeah right, teachers don't care about us."

Now, at 3:00 p.m., due to all the fights and commotion that happened on campus, parents are waiting anxiously at the gates to pick up their children. The school police have arrived and are patrolling the neighborhood. Several news vans have arrived, and reporters do their best to interview parents' students and faculty. I notice a gathering of members from a school reform group that are marching around outside; trying to convince parents that their children are not safe here, urging them to sign a petition to turn the school into a charter school.

I watch as the students exit the campus, and I began to reflect on my own traumatic experiences walking home from school as a kid. I start to wonder; "How can we help our students break free of the chains of poverty, violence, and systematic oppression that are holding our students back from academic success? How can we better motivate, educate, and inspire all of our youth to be the best students they can be?"

These questions along with many others were the inspiration for this book.

Teacher Journal

It's Back to School night! Lord, Help me! I already know tonight is going to be a hot mess because things have been absolutely crazy on campus the last few days. There have been what seems like a hundred fights this week and a lot of stress in the community. I think there has been a couple teacher - student altercations too. On top of that, my class has been a little out of control lately as well. Some students refuse to work with each other and have been very disrespectful to one another. I am going to have to figure something out, I can't go six more months like this. It's not even Halloween and I am starting to get frustrated with this job. I'm starting to lose my temper and patience with these kids. Somebody says one more thing about my mama, we might have a problem.

It's about four thirty and there are still four hours to go. Mr. G walks by on his way to the bathroom. "What's up Shaw" He yells as he hurries by. "How many you got so far?" "None yet," I yell, "but I think about five-thirty they will probably start rolling in."

It's five thirty, the principal and vice principal walk by to check on things. "How's everything going?" they ask, "I'm all good, I'm ready to go!". I point to the portfolios and grade sheets on the desk. "I'm ready for action! "Any parents so far?" "No, not yet," I reply. "Don't worry," the principal says, "right around six, some parents will show up, that's why we extended conferences to eight thirty to give parents more time to get here."

Six thirty, I can hear people passing by and I see a few families walking around outside. I set my novel down and prepare for my first visitors. "Hey Shaw," Mr. G walks by again. "You want a Coke or something?" "Nahh, I'm good. How many you got now?" He says. I responded slightly embarrassed and confused, "Ummm, none so far, I don't know what's going on?" "Yea, well that's how it is sometimes." He says, as he hurries off down the hall.

I am so deep into my book by 7:30 pm when a lady comes through my door, I am only slightly disappointed when she said, "I'm sorry, I think I am in the wrong room," examining the room over, "You don't look like a Mrs. Thomas." "Oh no," I laugh and direct her to the classroom next door. Shortly after, Ms. Brooks and Ms. J walk in, "It's time to pack up Shaw. We only have thirty minutes left. We ready to go!" "I know," I reply, "I'm ready to go too. I have been here since 7:30am this morning".

It's eight thirty! I'm packing up. Mr. G walks through the door with his bag on his shoulder. "90% of parents showed up tonight!," He says with a big smile on his face. "I still have to get that last ten percent though," he says. "I'm not happy till it's one hundred percent. Those last ten percent are the parents that you really need to speak to. How about you Shaw? How did it go? How many parents did you get?" I did not even bother to reply, I was too embarrassed. I guess parent engagement does matter. I guess all the emails, phone calls and letters home do make a difference after all.

Discussion Questions

1. Why do gangs and gang violence continue to thrive in urban communities?

2. How can we reduce violence on campus?

3. What can we do about violence in the community?

4. How do you promote peace in your classroom?

5. What is your plan to help encourage parent engagement?

Chapter Two

It's Past Time to Close the Gap

Ever since the landmark Brown vs. Board decision and the civil rights era, the United States has had to consider issues of quality and equal education for minority students. Nearly six decades later, after considerable political, financial, and institutional reform, an educational achievement gap still exists today. African American and Latino students continue to lag behind and be outperformed by their affluent Caucasian and Asian counterparts on national standardized test. Slightly less than three-fourths of African American and Latino students graduate from high school, and far fewer than that number enroll in and graduate from college on any level.

[1] This issue is especially critical for African American and Latino boys who are getting suspended and dropping out of school at an alarming rate. Even more disturbing, is the idea that our inability to keep our black and brown students engaged and inside the classroom is contributing to the awful school-to-prison pipeline phenomenon. The "school-to-prison pipeline" is best described as; the trend where students of color and from disadvantaged backgrounds are more likely to drop out of school and end up in the juvenile system or a correctional facility. Which in turn, leads to a negative impact on our urban communities and our society.

---

[1] DePaoli, J. L., Fox, J. H., Ingram, E. S., Maushard, M., Bridgeland, J. M., Balfanz, R., ... Alliance for Excellent Education. (2015). Building a Grad Nation: Progress and Challenge in Ending the High School Dropout Epidemic. Annual Update 2015. Civic Enterprises.

This phenomenon is an area of extreme concern, mainly for African Americans based on the fact that their arrest rate is significantly disproportionate in numbers. [2] As a result, the impact of men, (brothers, husbands, and fathers), missing in the home due to being in prison, is having a devastating impact on communities and families of color.

A tremendous amount of literature on the topic of teaching minority and low-income students is readily available in bookstores across America, but there is very little overall national progress in the area of successfully educating low-income urban and minority youth. Since the civil rights movement, policymakers, educators, political leaders, community activists, philanthropists, university researchers, and special interest groups have been seeking reforms to help close the educational achievement gap between low-income minority youth and their counterparts. Unfortunately, nearly sixty years later, we are still searching for answers.

Why has the American education system failed to equally and adequately educate students of color? Why have students of color not yet closed the educational achievement gap in America? These questions are deeply perplexing based on the financial implications it has on this country. It appears there would be huge financial incentives in educating students rather than housing inmates. On average, states spend about two to three times more a year to incarcerate an inmate as they do to educate a student.[3] Although the research seemed to indicate that per pupil spending does not show a strong positive correlation to improving student achievement.

[2]Aguilar, D. N. (2014). Oppression, Domination, Prison: The Mass Incarceration of Latino and African American Men. Vermont Connection, 35, 12–20.[3]U.S. Bureau of Prisons 2018 annual Budget https://lao.ca.gov/policyareas/cj/6_cj_inmatecost

I doubt many people would argue against the idea that our tax money would be better off spent on educating students rather than focusing on keeping our youth locked up. [4]

After what felt like an endless project of wading through a mound of research literature, I realized that the resounding conclusion that researchers made is to "hire great teachers" for improving the education experience of minority students in urban areas. Indeed, hiring great teachers could help begin to turn things around in urban schools, but simply hiring great teachers might not be enough to close the achievement gap. "Great teachers" are not the bottom line answer. School districts will need to be able to recruit, engage, and retain great teachers even to begin to start to close the gap effectively. Unfortunately, for schools located in economically distressed areas, recruiting and retaining great teachers is challenging for many obvious reasons, not the least of which is salary. It appears that the best and brightest college graduates don't want to work for the modest national $42,000 average starting teacher salary. [5]

After delving deeper into the subject, some research literature also indicated that providing additional training for teachers in isolation does not necessarily improve achievement in the classroom. Research suggested that a meaningful, collaborative professional learning community is necessary to make any significant and substantial change in student achievement. So, the conclusion is urban schools need to have great teachers working and training collaboratively for a significant period of time to begin to effectively close the achievement gap.

[4]Jackson, C. K., Johnson, R. C., & Persico, C. (2015). Boosting Educational Attainment and Adult Earnings: Does School Spending Matter after All? Education Next, 15(4), 69–76.
[5]Gaines, G. F., & Southern Regional Education Board, A. G. (2001). Focus on Teacher Salaries: An Update on Average Salaries and Recent Legislative Actions in the SREB States.

Surviving and Succeeding as an Educator in a High-Needs Urban Area

An "Urban area" is best described as a large, diverse, and densely populated region with significant infrastructure that is located in close proximity to a major city. Urban schools in such areas are generally described as being positioned within communities with high crime rates, poverty, large percentages of minority students, with limited English proficiency, and a large percentage of high-needs students.

The difficulties of being a teacher in a high-needs urban area have been well established. These factors include absenteeism, poor physical conditions of classrooms, lack of parental support, low teacher pay, misbehaving students, violent neighborhoods, lack of resources and supplies, lack of a strong learning culture, high concentrations of immigrant students, continuous shifts in curriculum or educational philosophy and a lack of counseling or administrative support. Teachers in urban schools feel the daily stress that comes with having to act as a; counselor/therapist, psychologist, nurse and social worker, in addition to teaching. The combination of these factors and stressful conditions may be most likely the reason nearly forty percent of all new teachers leave the teaching field for other industries within their first three to five years of starting the profession. [6]

Because you are reading this book, chances are you may be a new teacher or a veteran teacher looking for help. Possibly, you want to make significant academic, procedural, or behavioral changes in your classroom. Perhaps you are a concerned parent seeking to help your child become more successful in the classroom. Maybe you're an administrator or an instructional coach looking for additional strategies to share with your teachers. Whatever your own education emergency is, I created this book for you. The ideas, procedures, methods and strategies that I am sharing here can be used by novice and veteran teachers alike. No matter where you are in your journey as an educator - or life as a parent who wants more for your child, my hope is that this book will help you improve your students' overall learning experiences and daily life.

[6]Fuller, B., Waite, A., & Torres Irribarra, D. (2016). Explaining Teacher Turnover: School Cohesion and Intrinsic Motivation in Los Angeles. American Journal of Education, 122(4), 537–567.

My Teaching Experience

My teaching experience has been interesting, exciting and challenging thus far. I have spent the majority of my teaching career working in urban areas of southern California, including the Watts, neighborhood in South Central Los Angeles, and most recently in the historic "westside" Las Vegas area. I've worked in schools in low-income neighborhoods where many students, often from single-parent households, come to school hungry and may eat three or four school lunches because they do not have enough food at home. I've taught students who have been temporarily homeless, shuffled through foster-care, or sent to live with distant relatives. I have worked with students who suffer from depression or anxiety and students' whose parents have struggled with mental illness. I have also taught middle schoolers who read near a third-grade level. My experience includes teaching students who are worried about nuclear war. My experience includes working with students who are confused why black lives don't matter. My experience includes working with students who wonder how building the wall will disconnect them from friends and loved ones. My experience includes listening to students argue back and forth about whether we really need to make America great again. Some of the students I've taught live in constant fear of them and their families being deported, while others worry about gang violence or bullying.

My teaching experience has probably been very similar too many other teachers' experiences, with a lot of late nights and early mornings. I have lost weekends due to planning lessons and went without many lunches due to detention supervision. I have spent countless hours sitting in professional development sessions, making phone calls home or sending emails to parents. I have also spent an untold amount of my own out of pocket money on making copies or purchasing supplies for my classroom. I have also been to what feels like about one million IEP meetings.

My experience also includes working through budget cuts and working on campuses that are in desperate need of renovation and repair. I've taught lessons with textbooks that are out of date and science lab equipment that is missing pieces or obsolete. I've had the opportunity to meet some fantastic teachers, and some of those teachers that simply walked away. Not because they were terrible people, but because they could not handle the pressures of teaching in an urban low-income neighborhood—or were laid off because of a never-ending budget crisis. My experience includes working with teachers whose hearts are no longer in teaching but are too afraid to leave. I, myself, have experienced some days of incredible highs and demoralizing lows. There have been days that I have laughed until I cried, and days that I have just wanted to scream in frustration. I had enjoyed moments when I knew teaching was the only job for me and pushed through times when I felt that I could not last another week. I have encountered super-involved parents and parents who seemed utterly uninterested in their children's education. I have taught genuinely gifted students and unmotivated students alike. I have had the privilege of being supervised by supportive, encouraging administrators, and negative, document everything, punitive administrators as well. I know that every student, classroom, school, and community are unique. I may not have experienced everything yet, but I am confident that I have witnessed some of the best and the worst that urban education has to offer.

How Do We Bolster Academic Success for All Students?

As you may well know, there are some great moments in teaching, and I am sure you can relate. Some of my best experiences are observing students restating directions, having meaningful discussions, or watching students being kind to one another. The good days are when lessons go well, or witnessing a student overcome a challenge, or when the students express that they enjoy the class and enjoy having me as their teacher, it feels great to be an educator. Then there are the times when students are not engaged in the lessons, and when classroom management was not where it needed to be. The days when students are not respectful, or students did not show up to class. The worst moments have been the times when the classroom felt out of control, and a feeling of helplessness, defeat, and loneliness prevail. Especially when working in an urban, high-needs school, I am sure you've had your share of these experiences.

Upon reflection, both the failures and successes have had a major impact on my practice as an educator. The failures include giving up on challenging students, not developing effective procedures, being slow to grade papers or give meaningful feedback on assignments, not contacting parents about a student's behavior or grades, not making connections with students, not making positive phone calls home, not taking the time to learn students' names, not spending that extra hour to differentiate instruction, not encouraging parent involvement in the classroom, not learning about community resources or simply not holding high expectations for all students. It seems like the things that we are **not** doing can have the biggest impact on our instruction.

The successes include getting to know the student, understanding where they come from, building their self-esteem, diagnosing students' needs, building confidence and motivating them to learn, planning lessons that are rigorous and culturally relevant, helping students connect academic lessons to career relevancy, and helping them master academic objectives.

My constant goal is to learn from the failures and to build on the successes. My objective is to help students master curriculum standards and become proficient. I want to inspire my students to think about their career path and provide them with multiple opportunities for career exploration, by setting goals to get the most out of each student, regardless of whatever obstacles they may face in or out of the classroom. I hold high expectations for all my students and expect them to perform despite the many valid reasons they may have not to.

My desire to decrease the negative interactions I was experiencing with students led me to identify and compile these strategies to help create a more positive experience in my classroom. Learning from previous failures has helped me to reduce confrontations with students, raise scores, and provide a safe, secure, and positive learning environment in the classroom. That is what "Education Emergency" is all about.

What Is Emergency Education?

It takes a special kind of person to work in a hospital. In the emergency room, doctors and nurses must be able to think quickly and make fast life-saving decisions while staying calm under pressure. Every shift brings a wide range of patients with unpredictable medical situations. A quick search on the internet leads me to believe that an emergency room physician may see on average between 30 to 40 patients a day. These experts must be able to quickly and correctly diagnose, evaluate, prescribe, and treat patients with different symptoms, needs, and medical histories. That ability to handle diverse needs at a rapid-fire pace is what makes the emergency room team desirable and in high demand. Just like there is a constant need for emergency room physicians, America's urban and high-needs schools are in desperate need of emergency teachers.

Emergency education is the pedagogy dedicated to the diagnosis and treatment of sudden trauma, gaps, limitations, and challenges of minority and under-served students in urban areas across the nation. The practice of emergency education includes the evaluation, diagnosis, and recommended treatment for an individualized student by a coordinated team. Practicing emergency education is similar to practicing emergency medicine in that it can be extremely stressful and overwhelming. Much like the emergency room physician, the emergency teacher must make quick decisions and provide urgent care for their students daily. Emergency teachers must be able to correctly evaluate, diagnose, prescribe, and treat a variety of complex and unique student issues at any given moment on any given day. The emergency teacher, like their medical equivalents, will most likely toss and turn at night and lose sleep, continually thinking about improving their practice.

Teachers working in low-income, urban areas across the nation in areas like the District of Columbia, New York, Detroit,

Philadelphia, Los Angeles, Chicago, Atlanta, and many other regions face severe challenges in the classroom every day. These teachers, who are often new to the profession, are charged with the responsibility of educating students who may be dealing with trauma or other significant issues outside the classroom. Some of the most common problems these teachers must diagnose and treat include neglect, family structure, homelessness, hunger, lack of health care access, abuse, custody issues, learning disabilities, bullying, gang violence, drug use or abuse, alcoholism, teen pregnancy, poverty, or loss of a family member due to arrest or violence.

Unfortunately, these teachers are often called to perform these challenging tasks in sub-standard conditions. Many of the urban schools located in low socio-economic neighborhoods are physically rundown. Most lack the funding to provide necessities to teachers, including textbooks, supplies, or equipment. These sub-par conditions widen the education achievement gap, which, increases the career achievement gap, as well as the chances that students will experience emotional illness, unemployment or spend time in jail, prison or worse.

The career achievement gap is best described as the: Increased probability that low-income, urban, and minority students will not be able to qualify or attain high paying jobs especially those that require a significant amount of math or science knowledge. This consequence, due to the lack of access to quality education or specific skills, creates a deficit in income over the life of these individuals' careers when compared to their more fortunate counterparts. It's a reality that now makes emergency education a social justice issue.

The amount of trauma minority students experience growing up in poor, or crime-filled urban areas is another significant reason for the practice of 'emergency teaching.' According to the Center for Nonviolence and Social Justice, at Drexel University, the word 'trauma' describes experiences or situations that are emotionally painful and distressing, which can overwhelm a person's ability to cope. In the healthcare industry, trauma theory is the idea that people who experience psychological trauma are sick and in need of care and healing. The correlative point is, students who have experienced trauma in the past or experience it on a more frequent basis are also sick and require care and healing. Then, if they receive this specialized care, they may be able to cope and learn more effectively in the classroom.

The school-to-prison pipeline phenomenon also highlights the urgent need for emergency education. Blacks and Latino male students attending schools in high crime rate and high-poverty concentrated neighborhoods are systematically being pushed out of educational institutions and into the correctional system. And this is all caused from living in high-stress conditions faced with multiple challenges. They lack positive role models and are attending under-sourced schools with overcrowded classrooms inevitably staffed with inexperienced teachers. These are all factors that lay this path to prison for far too many minority students. This is a crisis in which "Education Emergency" is so desperately needed.

My experiences in education lead me to believe a school's poverty concentration and students' social-economic status are two of the most critical variables when determining academic success. Emergency education is an absolute requirement in schools with a high level of low-income minority students, located in neighborhoods with a high concentration of poverty.

Being an 'emergency teacher' means accepting that a sizable portion of students who attend schools in high crime or economically distressed urban areas are in need of someone (many "someones") to invest time, energy and resources into these students and their schools. Being an emergency teacher means looking in the mirror and coming to the realization that "you are" the intervention, and that you can make the most significant difference in a student's life. Essentially, a teacher serving in this emergency environment must be willing to sacrifice a considerable amount of his or her own precious time in order to help others reach their goals. Being an emergency teacher means making no excuses for lack of student achievement but recognizing the academic and social issues and attacking those issues with knowledge, care, and purpose. Being an emergency teacher means being willing to be a lighthouse for our urban youth; being a constant beacon of light and hope for our students to help them safely navigate in the right direction even through their darkest moments. Being an emergency teacher provides engaging, non-stop, hands-on, collaborative, inquiry-based, higher level, culturally relevant, materials, and lessons.

Every student deserves the right to a quality, college-preparatory education regardless of their religion, ethnicity, social-economic status, gender, sexual preference, or zip code. It is the responsibility of all stakeholders—parents, educators, administrators, community members, politicians, and business leaders—to fix the injustices and systematic lack of equity that low-income and minority students face particularly, in at-risk urban neighborhoods.

My goal is to provide new and veteran teachers in urban areas with effective remedies that can be used to properly diagnose, evaluate, prescribe, and treat students' needs. My hope is that this book *Education Emergency* will spark conversations that lead to professional learning communities to develop strategies to close the educational achievement gap, eliminate the career achievement gap, develop emotionally healthy and productive citizens, and disrupt the school-to-prison pipeline.

Included are some excerpts from my teaching journal to give a glimpse of a few of my most memorable moments inside of an urban classroom. Please enjoy these journals, but more importantly, please avoid some of the many mistakes I made in the classroom before I *woke up* and realized how important this work really is.

Teacher Journal

I'm not sure what happened. I just could not take it anymore. I was frustrated, and I just wanted to give up. The class was going crazy, and I felt like I was losing control. I don't know if it was the fact that grades were due at 3:00 p.m., the ten-page research paper that was due for my credential class by midnight, or the combination of it all. I felt really defeated. It was hot, my body ached, sweat was dripping down my back, I felt sick to my stomach and I had another pounding headache. My spirit was already breaking. It was sixth period and I was ready to go. The usual cast of characters were acting up more than usual today. I don't even remember what Melvin said that caused the class to burst out in laughter again, but I clearly remember how I responded to him. I just exploded, "Melvin, sit your fat, ugly self, down and shut up, so I can teach." The class went crazy! Cornelius ran around the classroom doing an impression of me over and over, each time getting more dramatic and louder than the previous version.

"I'm going to tell my dad," shouted Melvin. "So what?" I yelled back. "I don't care! You think I'm really still gonna be here teaching in the hood, five years from now when your dad gets out of prison." The class goes crazy again. Briana jokingly yells out, "Damn, your dads in prison too?" The bell rings and the kids run out laughing and taunting Melvin. I knew I had messed up, but I just didn't care anymore, I was mentally exhausted. I sat in my chair for a few minutes and then walked down to the library for professional development. One hour later, I headed to my classroom to pack up for the day. I sat in my chair for a few minutes and wondered how much longer I could do this job. My thoughts were interrupted by footsteps coming up the stairs and followed by someone pounding on my door. I paused for a second before opening the door to find Melvin and his six-foot-four-inch, two-hundred-fortyish pound dad standing there. Melvin's dad had on sagging jeans with red

bandanas tied around each wrist and tattoos on his face. I tried to greet him, but he wasn't having it. He quickly cut me off, "My son told me you want to disrespect him and his family, and you're some type of comedian. I wanted to meet you for myself and hear some of your jokes." My heart raced as I tried to downplay the situation and watched Melvin's dad grow angrier by the second. How did I get into this position? Where was everybody? How did he get by the front office and where was security? My hands started to tremble. I tried to explain how hard I was working, and that I made a mistake in calling out his son, but he dismissed me and turned to his son. "What did he say to you?" My heart went from a quickened pace to a low pounding. I knew there was no way out of this situation. I thought about running, but that would be an admission of guilt and would make me look like a total punk. Seeing how serious and angry he was reality was quickly setting in for me. I'm probably going to have to fight this guy and hopefully not to my death. When Melvin didn't answer, he yelled again at his son, demanding him to repeat what I said earlier in class. Melvin looked at me and then to his dad and said, "Nothing, Dad." The dad pulls a knife out of his back pocket and sits it down on the desk between us. Melvin looked up at me with a seriousness that I had never seen from him before. I nervously take a step back. I try as hard as I can to stand still and look unfazed. My heart now starts to bang in my chest, every single beat hits harder and harder, vibrating through every inch of my body. "What did he say to you?" He yells and bangs on the desk. Melvin, now with tears in his eyes, said, "Nothing, Dad. He didn't say anything, it was me, Dad. I was playing in class. I kept telling jokes, interrupting his class." Melvin's dad stood right in my face and gave me a cold hard stare and without saying a word grabbed his son and walked out. Melvin took one look back at me just before his dad pulled him out the room. I collapsed in my chair, trying to process what had just happened, sitting in total silence just feeling my heart beat: Boom, Boom, Boom, Boom, Boom, Boom…

Discussion Questions

1. What roles do teachers and schools play in disrupting the school to prison pipeline?

2. Why do some students seem resistant to giving it there all in the classroom?

3. Are urban minority or low-income students really at a disadvantage in the classroom?

4. What type of adverse situations are your students experiencing?

5. How effective are your Professional Learning Communities at your school?

Chapter Three

Evaluate

Much like an emergency room doctor, the emergency education teacher must be able to evaluate their students effectively. Assessing students is just a quick check to make sure your students are prepared and ready to learn. Students typically should have some learning materials and supplies. Do the students seem unusually upset or troubled? Evaluating students is all about just taking the time to give that little bit of special attention to every student. Does your student have a new backpack, hairstyle or a new pair of shoes? Taking time to be attentive to small details can make all the difference.

It is believable that students attending schools in at-risk neighborhoods might experience harmful or potentially hazardous situations quite frequently. Therefore, it is imperative that emergency education teachers continually evaluate and reevaluate their students to make sure they feel safe and secure enough to learn. You generally want to see students who are happy, healthy, excited, motivated, energetic, confident, and vibrant. Those characteristics show that children are joyful and ready to learn. Observation is part of triage — allowing you to determine which students are in need of emergency care. Here are five strategies to use to improve your evaluation skills in the emergency classroom.

Strategy #1: Be at Your Door

Excellent teaching begins before the students ever walk into the classroom. Stand at your door and be visible to your students. So many potentially negative things can occur around campus throughout the school day, but standing near the entrance can help to reduce some of these occurrences dramatically. When you stand at your door, you let students know that when they walk in, it's time to focus and learn. Seeing you helps put students in the right mindset for learning. Standing just outside your classroom also allows you to move kids along and encourage them to hustle and get to class on time.

The primary purpose of standing at your door is that it allows you the opportunity to evaluate your students. Pay attention to each student as they come through the door.

- Does your student have a backpack?
- Did your student bring supplies?
- Did your student come through the door appearing upset or excited and ready to learn?

By standing at your door, you may be able to remedy a problem before the students even step foot into the classroom. Besides, it allows you to purposefully and uniquely talk to each student. Again, this strategy will enable you to evaluate the physical and mental readiness of each student. It's also a time to remind students of your classroom rules and expectations.

Many teachers choose to shake hands with each student or ask them a content-related question as they come through the door. Some teachers like to add a personal touch such as, "Hello, Mary, are we ready to tackle those fractions today?" Other teachers use this time to give students instructions to have their homework out and ready or to open their books for silent reading.

Whatever you choose to do or say as you welcome students to your classroom, use this unique time to evaluate and connect with each student. It's a small moment to remind the student that you care about them and that you expect greatness from them today.

Strategy #2: Emotion Chart

Just as doctors and nurses in the emergency room must closely monitor a patient's condition for change, it is likewise just as important for the emergency teacher to be aware of any sudden change in status to their students' well-being.

Many teachers use an emotion chart to continually monitor and evaluate the mood, feelings, and attitudes of students in their classrooms. An emotion chart allows students to move a pin from one zone to another based on how they are feeling at the moment. Most teachers ask students to immediately move their pins as they enter the room to minimize disruption to the instructional time. Some teachers use a simple color chart of green, yellow, and red zones, while others use a more complex table of categories such as angry, frustrated, depressed, or happy. Some teachers have even included being sleepy, or hungry on their classroom mood charts. This strategy is most effective at the primary level but can easily be adapted for the secondary level as well.

Knowing which children may be dealing with issues on a particular day can give you a strategic advantage. It allows you to recognize emotional needs and refocus students on learning. As an emergency room teacher, your goal is to help students quickly move from being negative or upset to a calm or positive state, so they can continue participating in learning activities.

Strategy #3: Journaling

Journal Writing: The benefits of journal writing in the classroom have been well established. Journaling can be used to help improve students' penmanship, writing skills, and their ability to express themselves. It can be used at any point during a class period depending on the instructional purpose you are using it for on that day. Many teachers use journaling as an opening activity to help provide quiet time and to help settle students down. Additionally, journaling can be used to practice note-taking or as a quick check at the end of class to gauge students understating of a specific lesson.

The emergency room teacher uses journaling for all the previously listed reasons as well as to evaluate students. Provide journal prompts that are fun and encourage creative writing, that drive students to reflect on their own actions, choices, dreams, and goals. Using selective journal prompts, you can learn valuable and personal information about your students and discover how they feel about their social-economic status or social justice issues in their community. This insight may help you reach and teach your students in ways that are meaningful to them individually.

Journal Prompt Examples

1. What is your biggest fear and why?
2. Five things you may be surprised to learn about me are…
3. It is important to be a good person because…
4. If you could change one thing about your life what would it be?
5. Why is integrity important?
6. Three things that make me unique are…
7. If you could improve one thing about school what would it be?

8. The last time I was angry was…
9. The thing that makes me saddest is…
10. When I grow up I want to be…
11. Who is your role model?
12. When I feel stressed I…
13. Sometimes I get angry because…
14. Describe your experience getting to school…
15. When was the last time you experienced peer pressure?
16. Describe the members of your family…
17. Who is your best friend?
18. Would you consider yourself a good friend? (Explain)
19. Would you steal one hundred dollars if you could get away with it?
20. What is the best gift you have ever given or received?
21. If you could change one thing about the world…
22. I really hate when…
23. My favorite subject in school is…
24. My favorite television show is…
25. My favorite activity is…
26. I would like help with …
27. My biggest secret is…

Journaling is an effective evaluation strategy that can be used by every classroom teacher.

Strategy #4: "I Am from" Poem

An "I Am from" poem is a powerful expression of creativity that tells the story of where students come from, what major events have shaped their life, and what makes them unique. "I Am from" poems are powerful because they allow students to hear the stories of their classmates firsthand and make connections between themselves and the student author. Not surprisingly, this activity has become popular in schools as teachers use them to learn about their students and give them an opportunity to express themselves.

In the emergency classroom, having students write these poems can be a great way to evaluate students. Many teachers assign these poems at multiple times throughout the year with the purpose of seeing a progression in their students over the course of the year. The teacher is looking to determine how the class and curriculum has changed the student for the better throughout the year? Some teachers have students present their poems to the class. Others have students perform their classmates' work with the authors' names undisclosed. This method of performing the poem can be very powerful for building unity in the classroom as students learn the challenges and hopes they may share in common.

I am From Poem

If I tell you where I'm from

Would you come visit, would you stay?

Could you help keep me safe

And walk me to school each day?

I am from the city of Angels

South Central L.A.,

where wearing the wrong color

could make today a bad day.

Imperial and Avalon, 115th street!

Around the corner from a liquor store,

A drug house and swap meet,

I am from a city of broken dreams,

broken promises, and despair.

Going to school with students

with just too much to bear.

Just another kid

from a single-parent home,

trying to learn to be a man,

but with no father at home.

I guess ummmm, some things, I will just teach myself,

like how to treat a woman, play ball,

and believe in oneself.

I am from Verbum Dei High school —

a private school in the hood,

an all-boy Catholic high school,

where teachers did all that they could.

I have to dress like this? C'mon mom, why?

A cardigan, dress shirt, slacks, and a tie!?

I am from not giving up

in believing in my dream,

in believing getting out the hood

is an achievable thing.

I am from Cal State Long Beach

Studying sociology, earning a degree.

Thinking about my friends that didn't make it

And wondering what's so different about me.

-West Shaw

Strategy #5: Student-Interest Survey

It may seem like a simple tool, but a student-interest survey may be one of the best ways to evaluate your students at the beginning of the school year. A student survey can help you get to know your students better, which, in turn, gives you an advantage in teaching your students in meaningful and useful ways.

Student-interest surveys should be well planned, purposeful, and seek to get detailed information about each student. Your inquiry may include questions about students' family life, such as family size and dynamics. It can also include questions about preferred learning styles and favorite subjects as well as questions about sports, hobbies, and special interests. Additionally, a survey could include questions about student confidence, self-esteem, and fears.

The purpose of the survey is to gather valuable data about the students that may be used to help make connections to the content relevant and meaningful. You can also use the information collected from the surveys to determine if students may require any additional support or services. Do the study at the beginning of the school year and repeat it throughout the year to capture changing attitudes.

The five strategies covered in this chapter are useful tools to help you observe the students in your classroom. These are just a few examples, but there are many other options available as well. You need to feel comfortable and find what activities work best for you in your classroom. It is essential for you to observe and pay close attention to your students and recognize what may be hindering them from excelling in the classroom that particular day and understand what you can do to help them get them back on track.

Teacher Journal

"Caesar! Get out some paper and a pencil and do some work." I didn't yell, then, but the moment was coming. I knew this kid was going to be a problem from the moment he walked through the door. Every day it's the same thing. He just sits there, wearing that same Compton hoodie and doing nothing but stare out the window or fall asleep. His complete lack of effort drives me crazy. I know it's only a matter of time before the other kids start to ask why doesn't he have to do any work?

Caesar transferred in as an opportunity student, meaning he had been basically kicked out of his home school and sent to us for a chance at a fresh start. He's only a sixth grader but seems almost as big as a high school student—nearly six-feet tall and looks to weigh nearly 200 pounds. He has dark black hair and big brown eyes, and there's something about his eyes that have always bugged me. He always looks me right in the eyes and then ignores me. It's like he wants me to be a hundred percent sure that I know he hears me but is choosing to ignore me. It makes my blood boil.

After looking through his records, I learned that he had an individual education plan (IEP) and had already been held back twice. I keep trying to tell myself just ignore him; who cares if he does not want to learn. But I just can't let it go. I've tried to threaten him, I've tried treats and incentives, I've even tried the super-positive caring teacher routine. Nothing seemed to work.

That day, I had already made my mind up: Caesar was going to do some work. I know he hoped that I would kick him out, but he was going to have to stay in class and get something done. As expected, he came in with no pencil, no paper, and no supplies. I slammed a pencil down on his desk and threw down a brand new wide-ruled notebook. Caesar opened the notebook and began to get to work. Five minutes later, I passed by Caesar to take a look at his work and there was nothing on the paper but drawings. "Get out!" I yelled. "If you don't want to learn, stay at home, or ditch school, but stop coming in here wasting my freakin' time." He shrugged and got up and walked out like my words meant less than nothing to him. My anger intensified at his lack of concern. I followed him out of the classroom and into the hallway. "What in the heck is your problem? What is wrong with you?" I yelled, as I followed him down the hallway. He just kept walking, so I ran to get in front of him and cut him off. "What is your problem? This is my classroom and you are going to do what I say. You better start coming in this class, on time and getting ready to work. I'm tired of you, and I'm tired of talking to you every day. You haven't done crap since you got here. Get your mess together and get it right or don't come back. I don't want you here if you don't want to be here."

I think above all else the key to amazing teaching is self - reflection. When I reflect back over this interaction with Caesar, I know that I failed him as a teacher. I know I let myself down as well. Kids growing up in some rough neighborhoods are being exposed to so much violence. I was doing the same thing the bullies, bad cops, criminals and gang members, were doing to people in these communities, creating more violence. I realized that being just another teacher that got angry or frustrated or yelled or got verbally or physical abusive was not going to help Caesar like school any-more or make him want to try any harder. I knew I needed to do better. I needed to learn to teach without violence. I needed to learn to connect with my students. I needed to learn how to build relationships. I needed to be a better teacher.

Discussion Questions

1. How do you greet your students each day?

2. How do you handle students that might be having a bad day?

3. What kinds of counseling services are available for students at your school?

4. How might you incorporate journaling into your lesson?

5. How Could your students benefit from sharing I am from poems?

6. How will you work with the Caesar's in your classroom?

Chapter Four

Diagnose

Just as when doctors practice medicine, a proper diagnosis is crucial for emergency teaching. Often times students come to the classroom with a variety of ailments, deficits or needs. As mentioned earlier, some of the common issues urban students in high-needs areas commonly face include neglect, family instability issues, homelessness, hunger, lack of health care access, abuse, custody issues, learning disabilities, bullying, gang violence, drug use or abuse, alcoholism, teen pregnancy, poverty, or loss of a family member due to arrest or violence. It is extremely important for emergency teachers to identify whatever ailments and needs a student may have. A proper diagnosis of a student's needs can help you begin the process of getting a student the correct services or modifications he or she requires.

A misdiagnosis of a student can lead to costly learning and emotional delays or even academic failure. If a student is misdiagnosed year after year, he or she may never receive the proper services, and is likely to continue to struggle academically. And each year that the student fails to master the content puts him or her at greater risk of dropping out of school. Therefore, it is imperative that teachers who work in disadvantaged urban areas learn to properly diagnose their students learning, social, emotional, mental, spiritual, and physical needs.

Diagnose Learning Needs

In education, diagnosing learning needs often requires assessment. Assessments are given to determine academic growth of individual students, identify trends amongst a group of students, and to compare students to their peers across the district, state or nation. Most teachers are all too familiar with administering various benchmarks and assessments. But aside from mandated testing, there are some assessments that you can do in your classroom to help you accurately diagnose your students' learning needs.

Two common types of assessments given in the classroom are formative and summative assessments. Summative assessments are typically explicitly carried to determine a student's official score at the end of a unit. While summative assessments are beneficial in understanding a level of mastery of the content, it is a formative assessment that is most critical for the emergency classroom.

Formative assessments are generally tools that help teachers determine the next best course of action. Formative assessments are beneficial because they allow the teacher to adjust their teaching approach to improve learning instantly. By using formative assessments, you can determine which students and what percentage of students have a strong understanding of a lesson or standard. Formative assessments provide an opportunity to reflect on a lesson and think of new instructional strategies and new ways to approach the lesson again. Additionally, formative assessments allow you to give ongoing and immediate feedback to students who may be having difficulty with a particular lesson.

In emergency classrooms, students often lack or are lagging in the skills necessary to master specific objectives. The urban-classroom teacher needs to use formative assessments as a tool to observe and monitor each student's progress throughout a lesson. Checking for the student's understanding and then immediately adjusting lessons as necessary.

A few examples of formative assessments include the following:

- Questioning – Ask strategic well-designed questions periodically throughout the lesson.

- Journal Entries – Have students demonstrate their understanding of a concept by responding to a journal prompt of the day's lesson.

- Exit Slips - Have students write down the answer to a specific question before they walk out of the door.

- Four Corners - Have students respond to a question by moving to a specific corner or area of the room.

- White Boards – Students jot down answers on white boards and hold them up for the teacher to get a quick assessment.

- Thumbs Up or Thumbs Down – Have students hold up a thumb or up down to show whether they agree or disagree with a question or to show their level of understanding.

- Graphic Organizers – Have students create a graphic organizer such as a Venn diagram to compare and contrast a topic.

- Plickers – Ask students to hold up a plicker card to respond to questions and use an iPad to cell phone camera to quickly collect data.

In addition to using formative and summative assessments in the classroom, teachers working in emergency areas should familiarize themselves with the many assessments that can be used to identify learning disabilities or special needs in students. A variety of assessments for cognition, language, auditory skills, visual skills, motor skills, social, physical health, and emotional skills.

But, again, a misdiagnosis or missed diagnosis of a student's learning needs could potentially damage the child's educational experience. A student could spend years without receiving the proper accommodations or services they need, or even worse, can end up placed in a special needs program in which they never belonged in. Statistics show that roughly 20 percent of students who are placed in special-needs programs never leave the program, which means an inaccurate diagnosis can affect students' education for their entire school experience.

A disproportionate amount of African American males in urban schools have been labeled emotionally disturbed or learning disabled.[7] These special-needs labels, in particular, carry a stigma that can be very demoralizing and can have a tremendously negative effect on a student's morale, confidence, and self-esteem. The long-lasting effects of misdiagnosis make it critical for emergency teachers to properly identify students and take the corrective steps necessary for that student. The teacher should work hand in hand with all stakeholders, such as counselors, nurses, doctors, social workers, therapist, and psychologist, to properly assess and diagnose student learning needs.

Diagnose Social/Emotional Needs

Learning is a social process, and developing proper social skills is vital to student achievement. It has been generally accepted that students cannot thrive academically until their basic social and emotional needs are met, which means that, in addition to diagnosing learning needs, urban teachers must be able to diagnose students' social-emotional needs.

---

[7]Toldson, I. A. (2011). Editor's Comment: How Black Boys with Disabilities End Up in Honors Classes While Others without Disabilities End Up in Special Education. Journal of Negro Education, 80(4), 439–444.

To learn at the most effective levels, students must feel safe, accepted, supported, and be able to communicate, interact, and work collaboratively with their peers. Urban students who go to school and live in high-crime, low-income neighborhoods could potentially face a variety of dangerous or stressful issues on any given day that strip them of any sense of security or support. Likewise, living in dangerous conditions may inhibit their development of communication and collaboration skills, as they may feel forced to be independent or "grown up" at an early age. Although children can be resilient, prolonged and frequent stressful conditions may well be one of the causes of low academic achievement in urban schools.

Five Recommendations for Addressing Students' Social-Emotional Needs

One recommendation for addressing the social emotional needs of students attending schools in urban areas is lowering teacher turn over. Urban schools located in disadvantaged areas often experience a higher teacher turn-over rate. This frequent movement of teachers and staff results in students being unable to form meaningful, long-lasting relationships with caring adults. It would be a great advantage to the students if they were able to build safe, healthy, lasting relationships with adults on campus.

A second recommendation for addressing urban students' social needs is increasing the number of adults that students have access to on campus. Urban schools are generally much larger than suburban or rural schools at the elementary and secondary level. Urban schools could have more than a thousand students enrolled each year. Students have very little opportunity to get quality individualized time from quality caring adults, especially students who may come from single-parent or foster households.

Having increased access to positive role models would be a great advantage to minority urban students.

A third recommendation for addressing the social needs of students is providing full-time services of behavior and mental health professionals such as nurses, counselors, psychologists, and social workers. Having qualified social-behavioral health professionals on campus is a tremendous asset to students who may be struggling with various types of emotional or social needs. Having health professionals available would be a tremendous asset to students attending urban schools.

A fourth recommendation is to provide students in urban areas with conflict-resolution skills. All faculty, staff, and volunteers on campus should participate in ongoing professional-development training in conflict resolution for themselves in addition to learning how to equip their students with those skills. Everyone, regardless of where they live, needs these skills, but students attending schools in emergency areas with high occurrences of crime, poverty, and violence will most likely have more opportunities to use these conflict resolution skills.

The fifth recommendation is to use social-emotional teaching strategies in your classroom. Emergency teachers should incorporate social skills, such as conflict resolution and problem solving, into their teaching practice and curriculum as often as possible. Embedding social skills into the curriculum gives urban students additional opportunities to experience and practice positive affective social behavior. Additionally, including social skills in the curriculum gives teachers an opportunity for students to practice the skills they desperately need in their everyday life.

Diagnose Physical Needs

Diagnosing a student's physical needs is just as important as diagnosing his or her learning and social-emotional needs. A safe learning environment is critical for student academic success, but urban students are more likely than their suburban counterparts to report not feeling safe while at school or near their school community. Research studies suggest that urban students, especially those in high-poverty or high-crime areas, tend to be more likely to witness or be a victim of a violent crime.[8] To improve the learning experience, urban schools located in at-risk areas must make every reasonable effort to ensure the safe arrival, stay, and departure of its students. Furthermore, urban teachers should regularly check in with their students, encouraging them to talk to adults about any concerns and inform them of where they can go to seek help if necessary.

Aside from the external threats to urban student's experience, studies suggest that minority students attending schools in emergency areas are more likely than their suburban or rural counterparts to participate in unsafe or risky behaviors. [9] These behaviors could include ditching school, under-age drinking, practicing unprotected sex, participating in gang activity, getting into verbal or physical conflicts, and experimenting with drugs.

Urban students are also reportedly more likely to be exposed to more health risks than their suburban peers for reasons as simple as poor hygiene or limited access to health care options. [10]

[8]Norman, J. (2015). Young, Poor, Urban Dwellers Most Likely to Be Crime Victims. Social and Policy Issues 32(1) 12-15.

[9]Veiga Rodrigues, C., Figueiredo, A. B., Rocha, S., Ward, S., & Braga Tavares, H. (2018). Risky Behaviors on a Student's Population. Journal of Alcohol & Drug Education, 62(1), 46–70.

[10]Price, J. H., Khubchandani, J., McKinney, M., & Braun, R. (2013). Racial/ethnic disparities in chronic diseases of youths and access to health care in the United States. BioMed Research International.

Health and wellness are important for academic success. A sick or unhealthy student is more likely to miss school or be unable to concentrate and is therefore more likely to struggle academically than a healthier student. Because urban students, whose families are more likely to be near or below the poverty line, often do not have access to proper medical care, schools should make a concentrated effort to promote and teach health and wellness. As an emergency teacher, make part of your job informing students about all the community resources available to them and their families.

Reports indicate that a significant number of students attending urban schools, especially those located in disadvantaged areas, do not get the proper nutrition they need. [11] Students in these areas often do not have adequate access to the proper amount or type of food at home. We know that it is essential for students to consume the proper amount of nutrition and calories to be able to learn and perform at an optimum level. A healthy diet can help prevent health-related issues such as dehydration, poor bone health, eating disorders, and fatigue. The combination of missed breakfasts, skipped lunches, and non-nutritious dinners negatively impact academic achievement in urban low-income neighborhoods. Black and Latino households in emergency areas, and specifically those headed by single woman, are more likely to suffer from food insecurity. The limited food supplies some families do have, is often high in calories and void of significant nutrition which attributes to an increased risk for obesity and weight related diseases such as hyper-tension and diabetes.

---

[11]ERIC Clearinghouse on Elementary and Early Childhood Education, U. I. (1994). Children's Nutrition and Learning. ERIC Digest.

So many factors contribute to poor physical health in students living in urban areas. Aside from food insecurity and less-than-nutritious diets, these students often live in dangerous neighborhoods where parents are often absent for long periods of time because of work or a number of other reasons. As a result, these students may spend more consecutive hours watching television or on social media and be less active than their peers. Furthermore, urban students often deal with barriers to physical activity such as transportation, available play space, community violence, and lack of funding for programs and equipment.

Eating an unhealthy diet in combination with not getting enough regular exercise or physical activity can have a significant impact on body composition and self-esteem. The physical fitness level of urban students can impact a student's health and self-concept and could be a significant barrier to academic success. As teachers, we must do everything that we can to advocate for nutrition and health. We must evaluate the level of need in our classrooms. We must teach and model healthy habits. We must be aware of the available resources on our campus and in our community.

Diagnose Mental Needs

The mental wellness of minority students attending schools in at-risk urban areas is critical for their academic success. Students attending large urban schools, especially those located in high-crime, low-income neighborhoods could potentially face an overwhelming amount of problems, stress, and violence almost daily in school, at home, and in the community. Oftentimes, urban students dealing with mental health issues struggle with self-esteem, depression, stress, and anxiety, which in turn often start to cause academic or behavioral problems at home or in school.

Research literature suggested that minority students in low-income areas are less likely to get the mental health services or support they need for a variety of reasons. [12] Funds available for mental health services and professionals in urban schools are limited. But the reality is that even where these services are available, many urban youths purposefully avoid talking to counselors because of the negative stigma associated with mental health issues.

Urban schools, especially those located in emergency areas of need, should promote the psychological health of all students and their families. Urban schools should focus on providing resources to families about mental health services available in the community.

Diagnose Spiritual Needs

Contrary to popular belief, urban schools are responsible for fostering the spiritual needs of their students. For the purposes of this book, we are going to focus on five pillars that make up spirituality:

1. A sense of belonging

2. A sense of purpose

3. A sense of hope

4. An appreciation of beauty

5. A sense of peace and quiet

---

[12]Gamble, B. E., & Lambros, K. M. (2014). Provider Perspectives on School-Based Mental Health for Urban Minority Youth: Access and Services. Journal of Urban Learning, Teaching, and Research, 10, 25–38.

Students attending schools in urban settings often deal with violence, stress, and trauma on a daily basis. The constant exposure to these negative influences can have a tremendously negative impact on their academic success, self-esteem, and mental and physical health. A special interconnectedness exists between spirituality and physical and emotional health. When people are spiritually healthy or grounded, they tend to be healthier both physically and mentally.

To ensure overall wellness in your students, work to bolster their spiritual awareness. Introducing students to the five pillars of spirituality can really help to minimize the negative effects of the urban environment. Increasing awareness of spirituality can help give urban students some additional critical tools to help cope with stress, loss, and trauma.

Teacher Journal

Someone once told me that the number one rule for a teacher was to never let them see you cry. When I heard that, I remember thinking, I thought the number one rule was never hit a student. My next thought was why would I ever need to cry in my classroom? When would it ever be that serious? I never imagined then that I would cry in front of students. I was wrong!

I'm tired. I am mentally worn down and I'm spiritually fatigued. I cannot change these kids. The kids don't care, the parents don't help, and I hate my administrators. People keep saying the schools are bad and the educational system is broken. The schools are fine, it's the people who are broken. How can one person change thirty-five kids, when the kids don't even want to change. How can I overcome the problems, deficits, and frustrations that these kids are bringing into the classroom?

I sit down in my chair and think about the futures of my students. The kids laugh, talk and throw paper around the room. The noise is deafening, but it all just seems to fade away. It just kind of feels like I am in the eye of a storm. Some of these kids are never going to leave these projects, and some probably won't even make it to see twenty-one. Is this my fault? Am I letting these kids down? Am I a bad teacher? Why is this job so hard? Why is it so stressful?

Sometimes it feels like the pressure is just too overwhelming. I have a chance to help save African American and Latino boys, and I am failing. I have a chance to make a difference, but I can't reach them. I have a chance to change lives, and I am just not good enough. The tears just start to fall. I cannot hold back any longer. The frustration, sadness, anger, and embarrassment all come pouring out.

I have just broken rule number one.

Discussion Questions

1. What assessments might you give students at the beginning and throughout the year?

2. Are you familiar with the mental health services available at your school and surrounding community?

3. How often do you conduct formative and summative assessments?

4. Do you teach social and conflict resolution skills to your students?

5. How often do you encourage students to eat healthy and exercise?

6. What can we do to address student's spiritual needs?

7. How do you promote positive parental and family engagement?

8. What is your system for communicating with parents?

Chapter Five

Prescribe

In chapter three the purpose and importance of being able to evaluate students was established. Teachers looking for students most ready to learn should be looking to observe students who are happy, healthy and excited. Chapter four identified the significance of diagnosing students' specific needs. Teachers should be looking for any obstacles that are hindering a student from learning at an optimum level.

Once you have evaluated your student's academic needs and diagnosed any obstacles they may be facing, it's time to come up with a prescription – a solution or a recommended plan of action. It is not enough to simply be aware of our student's problems and needs, as an emergency educator, you must equip your students with the necessary skills, attitudes, strategies and resources necessary for students to not only survive but thrive in and out of the classroom.

Prescriptions for Learning Needs

Rx - Develop a growth mindset

Introduce students to the concept of a growth mindset. Create an anchor chart, model thinking for students or use graphic organizers to highlight examples between a fixed and a growth mindset. Help students to identify the gains and small victories.

Rx - Develop culturally relevant lesson plans

Take extra time to find or develop unique, deeply engaging and challenging lessons that are relevant to your grade, subject and student population. Use newspapers, social media or current events to help create lessons that will help capture student interests.

Rx - Deliver culturally responsive lessons

Deliver lessons from the student's perspective. Try to truly create a student-centered classroom that considers the students' interest, point of view and cultural references.

Rx - Differentiate instruction

Create powerfully effective lessons by changing the levels of taxonomy and learning modalities often. Give students the option to choose which method they would prefer to complete an assignment.

Rx – Practice restorative discipline

Consider a discipline plan that uses strategies that teaches respect, cooperation and responsibility within the classroom.

Rx – Conduct action research

Become familiar with the process of conducting investigations in the classroom to solve difficult problems or to better understand phenomenon occurring in the classroom.

Rx – Incorporate Hip Hop in the classroom

Provide opportunities for students to listen too, discuss, create or analyze hip hop in the classroom to inspire and engage students.

Rx - Administer personality test

Have student's complete personality test to help students learn about each other and create groupings based on homogeneous or heterogeneous personality types.

Rx — Promote the inquiry process

Introduce students to the inquiry process and provide opportunities to practice this process during class time. Use anchor charts and graphic organizers to help develop student's ability to develop and answer questions.

Rx — Assess students regularly

Practice including more than one formative assessment in every lesson. Make sure to include summative assessments in long term unit plans. Reflect on assessment data and use that information to modify lessons or as a signal to re-teach.

Rx – Teach high level thinking skills

Help cultivate students' ability to think by providing opportunities to analyze information, organize information, critique information and think critically.

Rx — Keep parents involved

Communicate frequently through various modes of communication and keep parents up to date on school events, services provided by the school, community resources, homework assignment or any significant behavioral changes with the student.

Rx – Develop a Partnership

Encourage parents or loved ones to spend a minimum of thirty minutes per day working with students on academic skills at home. Provide information on school and community resources for academic and parental resources.

Rx - Create learning goals

Teach students how to create and develop and monitor learning goals. Have students create weekly, monthly, quarterly or semester goals.

Rx – Connect learning to Careers

Introduce students to a variety of careers by industry and help cultivate student interest by showing connections between learning and career interest.

Rx — Student Success Team or Response to Instruction Team

Assess and monitor students often and refer struggling students to the student success team or the response to intervention team to create a plan of action to move the student toward academic success.

Rx — Collaboration

Allow students opportunities to work with various partners and both small and large groups as often as possible.

Rx — Build mental endurance

Work with parents to help students build mental focus by encouraging them to reach a goal of forty-five minutes uninterrupted study/reading/think time at home each night.

Rx — Provide tutoring

Find time to make yourself available for tutoring services for your students. Create a resource where students can find free or low-cost tutoring services in the community.

Rx — Build subject-specific vocabulary

Build students vocabulary by using flash cards. creating a word wall, using work banks, having a weekly vocabulary quiz, or a vocabulary word of the day.

Rx — Provide tools and strategies

Practice using tools in class such as agendas, binders, planners and calendars to help students stay better organized. Provide time for students to get reorganized weekly.

Rx - Incorporate games and competitions

Plan to include games and group competitions into your lesson plan to help booster student engagement as often as planning will allow.

Rx — Incorporate social justice or service-learning activities into the curriculum.

Find ways to make connections with learning to the community. Allow students opportunities to get involved in local agencies and community issues. Use local news articles or the internet to locate issues involving your local community.

Rx — Incorporate technology

Make learning diverse and exciting by incorporating as much technology as possible in your classroom and homework activities.

Rx - Provide examples

Show students several examples of quality work and explain expectations of work before starting assignments or projects.

Rx — Take notes

Continuously work on building student's note taking skills and show them how to build subject notebooks or folder to keep notes organized.

Rx — Foster positive attitudes

Use every opportunity to work on helping to build positive attitudes with students toward learning and education.

Rx — Speeches

Routinely watch commencement speeches and other powerful speeches and use them as a tool to generate conversations that motivate and encourage student learning.

Rx — Summer learning goals

Encourage students to keep learning during the summer break and help them to set learning goals.

Rx – Teacher journal

Keep a teacher journal and use it as a tool to reflect and make adjustments based on classroom behavior, experiences, student responses and interactions.

Rx — Student surveys

Conduct student surveys frequently to gage student's perception on their classroom learning experience.

Rx — Professional Development

Continue to seek out professional development opportunities and extended learning courses in an effort to try and master subject content knowledge and learn some fun new things.

Rx — Dress to impress

Dress in business attire to model professional dress, and to enhance students' perception of the teacher's ability, importance and status.

Rx — Seek Donations

Apply for grant opportunities to bolster supplies and to bring new, unique and meaningful learning opportunities to your classroom.

Prescriptions for Social-Emotional Needs

Rx—Help students begin to perceive themselves as scholars, thinkers and learners.

Rx—Create a sense of community in the classroom.

Rx—Establish a team building/teamwork culture in the classroom.

Rx—Provide an emotional and intellectual safe, respectful and secure learning environment for all students.

Rx—Learn every student's name and at least one unique thing about each student.

Rx—Teach students how to properly introduce themselves by smiling, making eye contact, having a firm shake, feeling confident and projecting their voice.

Rx—Allow students several opportunities to work collaboratively on assignments and activities.

Rx—Encourage students to participate on school teams and in school extra-curricular activities.

Rx—Provide warm, positive and encouraging words of support daily.

Rx—Teach students to use daily positive affirmations about success, achievement and self-esteem.

Rx—Alert the school counselor about students who have a sudden change in mood or behavior, often seem down, seem angry or have experienced a sudden loss or difficult situation.

Rx—Make an extra effort to build quality unique relationships with struggling students. Find time, such as during recess or lunch, to talk to and get to know your students better.

Rx—Teach anger-management skills and techniques to students.

Rx—Teach conflict-resolution skills to all students.

Rx—Promote anti-bullying campaigns on campus.

Rx—Introduce students to new positive role models.

Rx—Help introduce students to the practice of creating vision boards and life maps.

Rx—Laugh and smile with the students every day.

Prescriptions for Physical Needs

Rx—Establish rules, procedures and routines in classrooms in an effort to keep all students safe.

Rx—Encourage students to speak out against bullying and harassment.

Rx—Remind students of the importance of starting off the day with a good breakfast.

Rx—Encourage students to practice a healthy and nutritious diet.

Rx—Encourage students to get an additional sixty minutes of exercise after the school day.

Rx—Recommend students to get at least ten to twelve hours of sleep per night.

Rx—Encourage students to participate in school sports or intermural programs.

Rx—Remind students of the importance of physical health and safety and encourage them to avoid risk taking behaviors.

Rx—Compile a list of community organizations and food banks where you can direct students' families.

Rx—Keep a supply of nutritious snacks in the classroom.

Prescriptions for Mental Needs

Rx—Talk to students about the importance of mental health and help to dispel myths about stigmas attached to mental health.

Rx—Teach students stress management techniques.

Rx—Encourage students to talk with school counselor or psychologist or any trusted adult about personal issues.

Rx—Recommend students pick up hobbies to lower stress and anxiety.

Rx—Create a list of mental health resources in the school community.

Rx—Create a sense of awareness in students about signs of depression and create strategies for supporting students with depression.

Rx- Work with the parents and an instructional strategist to apply the best strategies for students with special needs or specific learning disorders.

Prescriptions for Spiritual Needs

Rx—Create a sense of community in the classroom.

Rx—Let each student know that they are unique and a valuable and important part of the class.

Rx—Help students discover a sense of purpose.

Rx—Utilize music, art and theatre in lessons and in the classroom.

Rx—Always speak positively and inspire hope in students.

Rx—Include stories of hope and persistence into the curriculum.

Rx—Help students discover a passion for helping others.

Rx—Introduce students to the concept of meditation.

Rx—Introduce students to the principles of yoga and tai chi.

Rx—Use every opportunity to develop your motivational-speaking skills.

Rx—Help students to realize that they are what they eat, drink, listen to and watch on TV.

Teacher Journal

It's 10:00 p.m. on a Saturday night, I'm headed out the door on my way to the airport for a midnight flight to the East coast. My principal is taking a group of ten teachers to New York and Atlanta to check out a pair of high-performing schools. First, we are going to spend two days at a dynamic turn-around high school in Brooklyn, New York, and then we will head to Atlanta, Georgia, for three days to observe an innovative middle school located in one of the toughest areas of Atlanta. The first semester is almost over so I'm excited about being out the classroom for a whole week but am skeptical that this experience will have anything to really offer me. I am just excited to get back and start my Christmas break.

***

I was wrong! These last five days have been life changing! The things that I have experienced over this past week have left me amazed and speechless. Everything that I thought I knew about urban and minority students growing up and attending schools in economically distressed neighborhoods has been challenged. My belief that only a small percentage of these students could be successful has been shattered. During this past week, I have seen not just one, but two urban schools doing what I thought could not be done. I have observed students who were motivated and excited about learning. I witnessed kids being polite, respectful and encouraging to one another. I listened to students describe in detail their dreams and goals for the future. I observed kids excelling in math and science classes. I saw kids engaged in lessons and completing rigorous work. I heard students asking questions, debating and participating in class discussions. I saw students working in collaborative groups and having meaningful conversations. I observed kids that were organized, focused, excited, and motivated to learn. I saw students that believed in themselves and were determined to be successful. I witnessed parents volunteering and students doing volunteer peer tutoring after school. I saw students, teachers and administration being successful despite the obstacles and without excuses. I saw a school effectively closing the achievement gap. I did not think this was possible. I have made so many excuses as to why schools serving poor kids of color could never be successful. I blamed the system, the budget, the parents, the students, the community. I believed that these issues were to be big to overcome, but I was wrong!

Discussion Questions

1. How can you help students develop a growth mindset?

2. Do you always remember to include differentiated instruction into your lesson plan?

3. How often do you plan lessons that allow students to use different modalities of learning?

4. What methods do you use to communicate with parents? How often do you try to reach out to parents and guardians?

5. How can you teach students organization and time management?

6. How do you introduce and review subject specific vocabulary to students?

7. How does your school handle the issues of bullying and harassment?

Chapter Six

Treat

Up to this point, Education Emergency established that students who attend schools in disadvantaged urban areas and in low-income or high-crime neighborhoods face tremendous amounts of violence, stress, and adversity, in their everyday life at school, at home or in their community.

The first few chapters argued that many of the issues students in emergency areas of need may face include neglect, homelessness, lack of access to nutritious food, lack of quality health care, physical or mental abuse, custody issues, learning disabilities, bullying, gang violence, drug use, alcoholism, teen pregnancy, and poverty. My research and my conclusions precisely determined that these adverse experiences could negatively impact students' learning, social-emotional, physical, mental, and spiritual well-being.

Chapter six covers the final step of the emergency teaching process, which is providing treatment and how to do so. Recap: It is the job of every parent, community member, teacher, counselor, administrator, specialist and support staff to help reduce the amount of stress, violence, trauma and adverse situations students are exposed too. Emergency teachers must possess the necessary tools and skills to help students heal and cope with exposure to adverse conditions. An Emergency teacher is a teacher who can effectively evaluate, diagnose, prescribe, and treat a student's needs in an effort to help give students a better chance to be more successful academically even under extreme conditions.

The best treatment for students who face adverse situations is for emergency educators, like you, to teach quality, engaging, culturally relevant, and culturally responsive lessons. Teach with a growth mindset, purpose, magic, enthusiasm, and urgency. Set high expectations, require discipline, and provide rigorous assignments. Teach with the positive character traits you want students to develop by being a role model your students can emulate. Be intentional about building community, instilling hope, demonstrating faith, and teaching with courage, resilience, and love.

Teach with Character Traits

I've previously acknowledged that teachers who work in disadvantaged urban areas have a tremendously difficult job and face a variety of challenges every day at work. Despite these obstacles, we are still responsible for developing proficient students to prepare them for the next grade level. In truth, emergency teachers must do more than teach to proficiency. Those of us who teach in an emergency area must also teach character traits and core values if we ever hope to break the cycle of poverty, violence, and despair.

Teaching character is just as crucial as teaching mathematics or English. Cultivating character development helps give students the supplemental skills necessary for real success in life. Regularly, students living and attending schools in high-risk areas may be exposed to plenty of negative influences. These students need teachers who will help them develop the positive character traits that will equip them to overcome challenges and the constant negativity that life exposes to them. Students need teachers who will live up to the responsibility of helping them become the best people they can be.

Teaching character traits builds students' emotional and moral development. Teachers working with parents and guardians can help students become self-confident and responsible citizens.

Teach Students to Be...

Ambitious, Brave, Compassionate, Confident, Considerate, Courageous, Dependable, Determined, Friendly, Generous, Helpful, Honest, Kind, Loyal, Positive, Polite, Reliable, Responsible, Trustworthy.

Teach with Community

Teachers working in high-risk areas must do more than build a safe and positive learning environment for their students; they must build a community of learners. In your classroom, make it a goal to foster a sense of community where people are connected, care for each other, learn together, and share common attitudes, interest, and goals. Building a community of learners means helping students understand how to care for and about each other, realizing that for all their differences, they are alike in many ways. By building a community of learners, you can help students focus more on their similarities rather than their differences.

Students who attend schools in areas of need can significantly benefit from being in a community of learners. Because they are more likely to witness or be the victim of physical, emotional, or verbal violence. Creating a classroom community can help students feel supported and connected. As they develop skills that strengthen relationships, such as conflict resolution, student interactions will improve, and classroom misbehaviors will reduce. At the same time, students' attitudes toward learning, each other, and themselves will improve as their confidence and motivation grow.

In addition to the teaching community in the classroom, emergency teachers must build strong relationships in the community. The emergency teacher must make a serious effort to include students' cultures, families, and traditions into the classrooms and the curriculum. Teachers should also try to be familiar with and be involved with local community organizations that could provide services and resources to students and their families.

Teach with Courage

There is no doubt that you need the courage to serve in a high-risk area. Teaching in an urban school—in some of the nation's toughest neighborhoods—requires that you inform without fear or hesitation. Emergency educators will most likely experience some challenges and most likely work under some of the most challenging conditions. You must not be afraid to think outside the box or do whatever it takes to help move children forward. This courage includes having the bravery to reach out to busy parents and challenge them to push their children toward academic success in a loving manner and not by use of threats or verbal abuse. Sometimes, teaching a student also requires teaching the parent too.

In addition to displaying courage, teachers must teach students how to be courageous themselves. Students face a tremendous amount of pressure and obstacles growing up and attending schools in emergency neighborhoods. Courage is one of the essential character traits that students in disadvantaged areas need to develop.

Students who face violence and stress must have the courage to succeed. Students might need the courage to be first in their family to graduate high school or be accepted into college. Encourage your students to have the courage to be different from their peers and friends and to say no to peer pressure and bad influences. Students must develop the courage to try and work hard when sometimes it is easier to give up.

Teach with Discipline

It is no secret that to make significant academic gains in any classroom; the teacher must first establish effective classroom management. By creating a positive, safe, and nurturing learning environment. Building this environment requires both the teacher *and* the students to be disciplined. In the emergency classroom, instructing students to be self-disciplined is critical because chances are, they are not learning this vital skill outside of the school.

Being self-disciplined is a skill that not only helps students in the classroom but will also help them in many areas throughout life. Such as jobs, sports, and relationships., (et, al.) The reason for teaching self-discipline in the emergency classroom is about far more than turning in homework on time; it's about learning to manage one's behavior and emotions. Teachers need to keep minority students in the classroom to help close the achievement gap. But minority students, especially black and Latino boys, are sent out of the school and suspended in alarming numbers for behavior issues. The bottom line is that if they are always getting kicked out of class, they cannot learn. Teaching self-discipline empowers students to control their behavior, enabling you to teach the content with fewer interruptions.

Teaching self-discipline requires that you hold incredibly high expectations for your students and yourself. Provide boundaries, structure, and consistency for students. Create procedures and daily routines in the classroom. Establish positively stated rules and clear consequences and enforce those rules consistently. Model appropriate behavior and practice how to handle situations appropriately with students. Be positive but firm when correcting behavior. Continuously remind students about making positive choices; acknowledge small improvements but do not over celebrate them because you expect the best from your students.

Teach with Empathy

Empathy is what allows people to make connections and identify with or understand another person's actions, concerns, emotions, feelings, or perspective. It is critical for teachers serving students in disadvantaged areas to teach with empathy. Students attending schools in emergency areas of need could potentially carry a tremendous amount of stress and trauma with them into the classroom. Teaching with empathy could help to minimize some of the obstacles that are created by the frustration that students carry with them into the classroom. Teaching with empathy calls for teachers to connect with their students and consider their experiences while teaching, designing lessons, creating rules and having classroom conversations. Teachers who practice empathy will be able to better connect and understand the students they serve.

As with self-discipline, teaching the skill of empathy is important. Now more than ever, teachers are responsible for moral and intellectual development. Teaching students how to practice empathy can greatly improve the classroom experience. Students will learn how to identify and communicate their emotions with peers. Students will learn how to identify with others' feelings and make connections with one another. Practicing empathy can help improve relationships, promote a positive environment and contribute to that sense of community you desire for your classroom.

Teach with Enthusiasm

Enthusiasm is an infectious condition that affects student motivation and can be spread quickly and easily from one student to another. Enthusiasm is often referred to as one of the most important qualities an affective teacher can have. Therefore, it is imperative for all teachers especially those working in emergency areas to teach with enthusiasm.

Teaching with enthusiasm means; teaching with energy and passion, all the while making learning fun. As your excitement for leaning inspires students, your enthusiasm will help keep students engaged and help to reduce negative classroom behaviors. Students who frequently face trauma or stress in their community can easily be preoccupied or distracted during class time. As an emergency teacher, you must go above and beyond to keep students interested, engaged, and energized. Teaching with enthusiasm will help students to get excited about learning and improve student achievement. And remember, enthusiasm is contagious so the more positive enthusiastic energy you give out is what you will get in return.

Teach with a Growth Mindset

The concept of a growth mindset was developed by Stanford University Professor, Carol Dweck. Her work sparked a movement that is changing the way educators teach, and students learn. Teaching with a growth mindset assumes that a person's learning ability can be developed and cultivated. The contrast is a fixed mindset, which implies that learning ability is finite.

Unfortunately, many students growing up in distressed urban areas have developed a fixed mindset. Students' experiences inside and outside of the classroom have taught them to believe that their learning ability is predetermined or stagnant. With a fixed mindset, students feel that they are either born intelligent or not. Students who possess a fixed mindset are often entirely dependent on others for their learning. Students who have experienced adverse situations, negative classroom interactions, or negative stereotypes may be more at risk for developing a fixed mindset.

Surprisingly, people may be completely unaware that they even hold these fixed mindsets. Because students who have developed a fixed mindset may be more likely to give up on school and less likely to believe that academic success is possible. Urban teachers must work to instill a growth mindset, and that begins by teaching with a growth mindset. Believe that each student is capable of learning and achieving. Help students see that their learning potential is not fixed but can always be strengthened and developed. Teachers must help their students believe that there is no limit to a persons' ability to learn.

Emergency teachers must help students comprehend that dedication, persistence, resilience, and hard work are some of the tools necessary for developing their learning skills. Fostering a growth mindset is a powerful action for treating learning needs.

Teach with High Expectations

From the moment students walk into your classroom, it must be clear that you hold the highest of standards for all your students. Doubt and cynicism can easily sneak in, so you must hold yourself accountable to this standard of high expectations by being willing to be brutally consistent in what you ask for from students every day.

In the emergency classroom, holding high expectations means not lowering academic expectations for any student, including special education, minority, English language learners, or students who live in poverty. Maintaining high expectations means putting forth a genuine effort to set high educational standards for all students despite their race, gender, first language, or social-economic status. Holding high expectations means helping every single student establish a positive growth mindset.

Holding high expectations shows students you care about them and will hold them accountable for their learning. By contrast, a teacher that sets a low bar hinders students' progress by limiting the students' access to a high-quality education and, as a result, reduces the possibility of these students ever qualifying for higher level education opportunities.

One of the most significant aspects of holding high expectations for all students is believing that every student can achieve some level of academic success. That doesn't mean that every student must reach the same level of success, but every student must try to climb the ladder toward achievement.

Teach with Hope and Faith

Hope is not something we can see or touch, but it is something that we must all possess. When it comes to emergency education, hope is the fuel that enables a person to overcome obstacles and achieve academic success. Every teacher working in disadvantaged urban areas should be working to cultivate this powerful tool to increase student motivation and achievement. It is believable that students, who are hopeful, tend to achieve greater academic success, have lower levels of anxiety and depression, have healthier friendships and are less likely to drop out of school.

It is easy to understand how students who experience negative classroom interactions or students who continue to struggle academically could be growing less hopeful every day. When those frustrations are combined with discouraging factors, such as poverty or dealing with stress or violence, students are at risk for losing all hope for achieving success—academically or otherwise.

As an emergency teacher, you cannot let students lose hope. Stress the importance of having hope and seek to empower students with the tools necessary for cultivating hope. Along with a growth mindset, essential tools for cultivating hope include persistence and goal setting. Help students set goals and benchmarks, and when they have their eyes on a goal, provide them with strategies, resources, and encouragement so that they become successful in obtaining that goal. Maintain your belief, and theirs, through setbacks, to develop their level of persistence. Help them see failures as an opportunity to learn from their experiences.

Seemingly inseparable from hope is the principle of faith, the belief that students will overcome setbacks and challenges to achieve academic success. Faith roots itself in past experiences. A student practicing faith recalls past obstacles or experiences of failure and remembers that they overcame those challenges. Emergency teachers must help students become aware of the cycle of facing obstacles, experiencing setbacks, and overcoming challenges. Students who practice faith are less likely to give up because they believe very strongly that they will find a way to overcome new obstacles and achieve success.

Teach with Love

"Love is patient, love is kind. It does not envy, it does not boast, it is not proud. It does not dishonor others, it is not self-seeking, it is not easily angered, it keeps no record of wrongs. Love does not delight in evil but rejoices with the truth. It always protects, always trusts, always hopes, always perseveres". (1 Corinthians 13:4)

If you want to make a real difference in your emergency classroom, you must not only love teaching, you must love your students as well. Students in low-income, high-crime areas could be potentially coming to school hungry, stressed, angry, depressed, frustrated, confused, scared, neglected or abused. They are at risk for being bullied or mistreated and are more likely to be exposed to or be the victim of a violent crime or gang violence than suburban students. Furthermore, a significant portion of these at-risk students are being asked to take on adult responsibilities by their parents and are being forced to grow up to quickly. Because they are constantly being bombarded with peer pressure and negative influences, we must teach with love. Love is the counteragent that empowers students to function at their highest level.

One of the best things that we, as urban teachers, can do to help our students succeed is love them. We can show love for our students by showing up every day and giving it our all. We can show love by caring for our students and establishing safe and secure learning environments for them. We can show love by helping students feel special and unique. Urban teachers can show love by being patient kind and understanding in the classroom and by being positive and supportive of students individually. We can demonstrate love by spending free time with students during lunch or after school.

Show your love for your students by motivating and inspiring students to strive for academic excellence. Maintain high expectations for them to help them build their confidence and self-esteem. Teach them to love and care for themselves. Constantly encourage them to never give up and remind them that tomorrow is always another opportunity to try again.

Teach with Magic

Every urban teacher must become a magician and learn how to teach with magic. Teachers working with students who are less than motivated, stressed, frustrated or disinterested in learning must learn how to bring a sense of awe and excitement to the classroom. Students should come to school every day wondering, just what might happen today? We must always be ready to pull a rabbit out of a hat, make a coin disappear or produce a great lesson out of thin air.

There are many ways to teach with magic. One of the best ways to teach with magic is to bring music into the classroom. There is something about music that brings people to life. There is something about rhythm and the bass that sparks a light in my African American students especially. There is something about the brass horns and the percussion in Latin music that makes my Latino students excited and filled with energy. There is something about hip hop and reggaeton that both my African American and Latino students absolutely enjoy and cannot get enough of. Find a way to bring music into the classroom and teach with magic.

Another way to teach with magic is to bring the art of dance into the classroom. There is something spiritual and amazing about dancing. Dancing has deep cultural roots in both the African American and Latin American culture. Dancing is vital because it allows students a chance to be unique and express themselves. Dancing allows students to be collaborative, burn energy and become creative. Dance also allow student to make cultural connections. Incorporate dance into your classroom and teach with magic.

A third way to teach with magic is to incorporate stories. There is something special about listening to a great story. A good orator can hold an audience captive and make time stand still. A great story can take students away on an adventure without ever leaving the classroom. Stories are powerful because they can help students make connections, learn traditions and understand differences in cultures. Incorporate stories into your classroom and teach with magic.

There are many ways to bring magic into the classroom. Just like every magician each teacher must bring their own special set of skills with them to the classroom. It does not matter if you use art, music, dance, jokes or games. What is important is that you bring whatever abilities, skills or special talents you have with you to the curriculum every day. When you complete your lesson plan for each day make sure you ask yourself how am I teaching with magic?

Teach with Purpose

Every teacher working in disadvantaged neighborhoods, serving urban or minority youth must teach with purpose. Teaching with purpose is considering the who, what, when, where, why and how we must teach. We must be absolutely clear and focused on our purpose each day that we are in the classroom. We are only performing at our highest level when the purpose of our academic instruction is clear to the parent, administrators, teacher and the student.

Teaching with purpose means knowing who your students are. Teachers must make every effort to know their student's strengths, limitations and challenges academically and socially. Teaching with purpose means understanding what students should be learning. Teachers must be aware and make decisions about what standards and objectives need to be covered throughout the year. Teaching with purpose requires teachers to consider when instructional material should be covered when to move on with instruction or when to reteach. Additionally, teachers need to be aware of the present day political and community climate as well. Teaching with purpose means understanding where you teach. Teachers need to have an understanding of their school community and have an understanding of the challenges and resources of that community. Teaching with purpose means knowing why we are teaching what we are teaching and helping your students understand why we are learning what we are learning. Teachers must help make the learning relevant and exciting to the student. Most importantly the teacher must help the student to understand why this knowledge is useful and important to them. Finally, teaching with purpose is knowing how you are going to teach your students. Teachers must plan, assess and use data or student feedback to determine the best instructional strategies to deliver lessons.

Teach with Resilience

Resilience is a person's ability to adapt or recover quickly and easily from challenging or stressful situations. If you are an emergency teacher, you need to be psychologically and emotionally resilient. Teaching and living in emergency areas of need can be extremely stressful and can take a toll on teachers' mental, physical, and emotional health. Intense challenges are one reason teacher turnover in urban schools is so high. To best serve your students you must cultivate your own mental and emotional resilience. Urban teachers must be able to bounce back and quickly recover from frustrating, stressful or emotionally taxing days.

Building resilience in teachers can help keep teachers in the profession serving urban students longer.

Just like so many of the other character traits and skills you need to teach in an emergency classroom, not only do you need resilience, your students need this vital skill as well. Research suggests resilience is a key variable in improving students' academic and social skills [13] Teachers working in underserved areas can help to develop resilient students by creating positive, supportive learning environments and by providing students the necessary tools to respond positively to challenges when they arise. Developing resilient students can help improve the classroom environment and promotes academic achievement, self-esteem, and positive relationships.

Teach with Rigor

Sadly, year after year, millions of urban and minority youth graduate from high-schools across the nation inadequately prepared to complete college-level coursework or enter the professional workforce. Schools continue to give diplomas to students who are simply not college or career ready, and in so doing leave low-income and minority youth without the proper skills to overcome the significant disadvantages they face in life.
In response to this tragedy, lawmakers developed the No Child Left Behind Act, which was replaced by the Every Student Succeeds Act, which helped lead the way for the national common core education standards and the college and career-readiness state standards. The adoption of these initiatives has led to a call for teachers to teach with an increased amount of rigor in the classroom.

[13]Williams, J. M., Greenleaf, A. T., Albert, T., & Barnes, E. F. (2014). Promoting Educational Resilience Among African American Students at Risk of School Failure: The Role of School Counselors. Journal of School Counseling, 12(9), 1

Academic rigor combines instructional strategies that are purposefully used to help students think at a higher cognitive level and make the learning experience unique, meaningful and challenging. Rigorous learning activities often require students to think independently and complete multiple steps within a specific allotment of time. Rigorous assignments might require students to compare and contrast, hypothesize, group or organize information, synthesize or summarize information, critique information or create high-level questions about text or pictures.

Teach with Role Models

Role models can have a positive or negative impact on students' lives. As emergency teachers, we have the responsibility to provide positive role models for students to look up to, such as people who are successful and display positive character traits and a strong work ethic.

Students living in emergency areas are exposed to a significant amount of negative influences from a variety of sources such as peers, family, social and digital media on a frequent basis. A role model can be a positive influence, providing a living blueprint to guide students through life.

Exposing students to role models who come from their same community, are of the same gender or ethnic group can help cultivate hope in students. Having the opportunity meet minorities who are successful with great careers can be exciting, motivational and inspirational for urban minority students.

In addition to exposing urban students to role models every teacher working in a high needs area must be a positive role model. You have the power to be a positive influence and make a significant impact on students' lives. Be intentional about leading by example. Your success inspires, challenges, and motivates students to be the best people they can be. Model positive character traits, possess strong core values, demonstrate a strong work ethic, and advocate for academic success.

Teach with Urgency

Students of color, especially those attending schools in low-income urban neighborhoods, are routinely being outperformed by their affluent counterparts in our nation. Closing this educational achievement gap requires that every teacher serving in a high needs area should be teaching with urgency. Teaching with urgency does not mean rushing through the curriculum. Teaching with urgency does not mean to create a tense or stressful environment. Teaching with urgency means helping students realize that every hour in the classroom is precious. Teaching with urgency is a teacher's constant desire to keep students moving forward. Teaching with urgency is having a game plan and training with a purpose. Teaching with urgency is putting education in a historical and socio-culture context for students, so they understand how critical it is for students of color to become academically proficient. Teaching with urgency is making students aware that education is one of the primary keys to success and can change their socio-economic situation. Teaching with urgency means helping students see education through a social justice lens. It is assisting students in realizing that their academic achievement is part of the contribution necessary to create change in their community and around the globe. Students attending schools in urban, low-income, and disadvantaged neighborhoods are experiencing an education emergency. Therefore, teachers working in these areas should be working with the same sense of urgency as doctors in the emergency room.

Teacher Journal

I did not think that I could do another year in the classroom. I was ready to give up and walk away. I did not believe that I was making a real difference with my students in the classroom. The job was just too tough and unrewarding. I figured that I had completed my share of community service. I was going to spend my summer looking for a new career. But I can't quit now! The observation experience at these two schools has helped to motivate and inspire me. I am reenergized, focused and ready for the challenge. I saw with my own two eyes that it can be done. I can make a difference! I am going to make this work. I am going to make a difference!

Discussion Questions

1. How do you build a sense of community in your classroom?

2. Are the rules in your classroom fairly and consistently?

3. Do you teach with empathy in mind?

4. Are you teaching with enthusiasm?

5. Do you hold high expectations for yourself and your students?

6. Do you speak about the power of hope and faith in your classroom?

7. How do you know if your lessons are challenging or rigorous enough?

8. Do you include teaching about role models and character traits in your lessons?

9. How can help students become more resilient?

10. How does teaching with love look like in your classroom?

Chapter Seven

Growth

Teacher Journal

I have made a decision. My second semester is going to be better than my first. The rest of my teaching career is going to be better too. Our plane is waiting in line on the run-way at Hartsfield - Jackson airport in Atlanta. There is a line of about eight jets in front of us waiting to take off. I am so anxious, I can hardly sit still. My mind is racing, and my head is spinning with the possibilities. I am looking over what seems like hundreds of notes that I have taken down over the past week. I need to get everything organized. I have so much work to do. I need to get home, so I can start planning and preparing my classroom. What is taking so long? Let's get this plane in the air already! The moment these students walk through the door, I want them to know that things are going to be different. I need them to know that I am going to be different. We are all going to be different. Everything is going to be different.

Teacher Journal

I think it was somewhere over Texas when the doubts began to creep in. What is it about doubt anyway? Where does it come from? Is it always lurking outside like a mosquito just waiting to get in or is it always within us like a memory just waiting to resurface? It is Christmas time, how am I going to make any significant change to my classroom over the holiday break? I don't have the talent, skill, resources or the money to pull any of this off. Maybe, I should just wait till summer and focus on the next school year. No! No! No! We can't afford to waste another semester, another month, another week, another day. We cannot lose any more time. I have to move these kids forward. I need to create a motto, a mantra! I need some affirmation that helps to drive me forward when I am discouraged or tired and feel like I'm out of gas. I need an affirmation that represents us as a class and what we are trying to accomplish. I need something that helps students understand that there is nothing harder than hard work but there is nothing more satisfying than working hard. I need them to know that hard work pays off. Wait, That's it! Hard work! - Pays off! I can picture it now, A call in response! Hard work - Pays off! Hard work - Pays off! Hard work - Pays off! I like it!

Teacher Journal

Today is the day! I'm back home and ready to get working in my classroom. I am motivated but not exactly sure of my plan of action. I am back on campus walking toward my classroom. I stop at the classroom door and try to imagine my student's experience. What can I do to make their experience better? I decide in that moment that I'm going to interact with every single student that comes through the door. I am going to high five, shake hands or fist bump every child in line. I am going to speak to each and every student and call them by name. More importantly, I am going to celebrate my students coming to class. I want them to know that I am happy to see them. I need them to feel welcomed, accepted and loved.

Teacher Journal

As soon as I walked through the door, I knew what I had to do. I had never decorated my classroom door in all my years of teaching. I am not an artsy - crafty type of person, so I would avoid it at all cost. Every year I would see other teacher's doors and pretend to be unimpressed. Every year I would say I was too busy actually teaching to be worried about door decorating contests. I know there are a hundred other things that are probably way more important than this, but nothing is more important than this to me at this moment. This is an obstacle that I have to get over. This is a small test that I have to pass. I feel like if I can accomplish this, then I can accomplish anything in this classroom.

****

I can't believe that took so long. Now I see why I avoided this for so many years. It took me two and a half hours to decorate two doors. I am so proud of my work though. One door is covered in black butcher paper and has strips of red, yellow orange and green paper which look like fireworks and says new year, new you. The second door is also covered in black and has red letters that says hard work - pays off! I am exhausted! I think that's it for today. I stand in the middle of the room looking at both doors. I did it! I think I can do this!

Teacher Journal

I'm home watching my favorite couple on HGTV. I don't know why I love these home renovations shows so much. I can't help but to think about my classroom. Can I put shiplap up in my classroom? Is country chic still in? Can teachers install bamboo flooring without permission? Can I afford an interior designer? Are classroom designers even a thing? Should I create a classroom design business?

****

I had never put an ounce of effort into decorating a classroom. I strongly believed that real teachers, working in real areas of need, had more important things to focus on instead of classroom décor. I would laugh when I saw these teachers on Pinterest, Twitter and now Instagram and Snap Chat posting their colorful classrooms with matching throw pillows, lavish rugs and color coordinated bean bags, baskets and

98

posters. I was certain none of that helped bring up test scores, master content, change lives or helped kids get out of the hood. I just did not get it! Maybe, I had the wrong attitude. Now, I think I understand. Decorating the classroom is an expression of love. Taking the time to make the room nice is showing the students that you care about them and lets them know that they are important. I used to say that this is not a competition and people were focused on the wrong things. But, maybe it is a competition. Maybe, it's a competition of love. Maybe people decorate their doors, paint their walls, create over the top anchor charts, and buy cozy rugs to show the students and their families how much they love them. Maybe great teaching is always competing to show how much you love your students. I have not been doing anything to show my students how much I loved them. Well, that is about to change! I think I have figured it out, teaching is love.

Teacher Journal

I feel like an artist. I stand back and look at my room like a blank canvas. I dip the roller brush in the fresh white paint and start to roll over the dingy yellow stuff that had previously covered my classroom walls. As soon as I completed my first roll of the brush, I know there is no going back. I sit the roller down, turn my playlist to 90's R&B, turn the speakers all the way up, and get into the zone.

****

I feel a change in me. With every roll of the brush, I feel more confident, more excited and more driven to be a better teacher. It feels like as I slowly transform this classroom, I am slowly transforming myself. I roll the brush, I can do this! Another roll of the brush, I want to be a better teacher. I am making changes! I am going to have a better attitude. I am going to be patient. I am going to be kind. I roll and I roll and I roll until it is done.

****

I am so proud of my work today. The classroom looks amazing with the fresh white paint and recently buffed black tile floors. I am extremely proud of the pop of color, I added by covering my bulletin boards in red butcher paper. I can't help but stare at my newly decorated doors. I look around the room and dream of the possibilities. I imagined the kids raising their hands and being excited about learning. I consider changing the desk out for tables in order to improve collaboration but that will have to wait until another day. I will have to pray on that one.

Teacher Journal

I cannot believe that I spent so much money on my classroom today. I spent over two hundred dollars and that was just in Target. They should not call it the dollar spot if things in there are more than a dollar! I spent my whole day searching for things in dollar tree, Walmart, the teacher supply, Barnes and Noble and Target. I spent too much money, but my classroom is going to look great. I got all kinds of great things for my room. I found all kinds of cool coffee mugs to decorate my desk with, which is odd because I hate the taste of coffee. I found some nice black and red trays for students to put their work in. I found some black buckets that I could fill with supplies as well. I got tons of markers, pencils, pens, high lighters, paper, color pencils, composition books and glue sticks. I got a ton of colorful poster boards to help my anchor charts pop out against my new white walls. I picked up some bright cut out letters for my bulletin boards and a few Diary of a wimpy kid books to add to my classroom library. I am super excited about the class set of white boards and dry erase markers I picked up too at dollar tree also.

Teacher Journal

My classroom looks great. I have just finished changing out the desk for tables and the recently buffed black floors paired with the black chairs and the fresh white paint looks amazing. The red posters and bulletin boards give the room the perfect dash of color. The black and red trays and bins were the perfect choice for my room. I stand in the center of the room so I can look at both of my newly decorated doors at the same time. New year, New you! I keep saying to myself! Hard work pays off, I freakin love it! I can do this!

Teacher Journal

My room looks nice, but now I have to focus on me. What am I going to do to be better? What are my rules, procedures and progressive discipline going to look like. I did not even establish any real rules the first half of this school year. I need to create a better system. I want to create a system that works for me and my students. I close my eyes and try to visualize my classroom. I picture a student getting out of their seat to go to trash can. Ummm, excuse me I say, there's a procedure for that. I imagine a group of students rushing over to the lap top cart. Oh I'm sorry, there is a procedure for that too. I visualize thirty students all trying to grab color pencils at once. Yep, I'm going to create a procedure for that, I say out loud to myself. I pull out a yellow note-pad and jot down a few ideas. I walk around my room trying to think of new rules and procedures that I want to implement.

Teacher Journal

If you fail to plan, you plan to fail. I have always heard people say this, but I had never applied this concept to my own teaching. I guess that could explain why I have not had any continued success in my classroom. I have never liked to lesson plan and I think the quality of my lessons have suffered because of it. I need to create a routine for making time to plan. I want to deliver great lessons and implement more effective instructional strategies in my classroom. I guess the secret is in the sauce like they say. If you want students to be engaged and excited about learning you have to create engaging and exciting lesson plans. I am going to do more activities, group work and competitions from now on. I know there is a group of teachers that meet at the local bookstore every Sunday. I think I will have to give it a try. I am also going to commit to staying after school every Friday to grade student work. They say there is no greatness without sacrifice.

Teacher Journal

How will you use data to better drive your instruction? I keep looking at the words written on my last teaching evaluation. My eyes keep shifting back and forth from those words to the big box checked needs improvement right next to it. I guess I can't lie to myself. I know I haven't been using any real data to help guide my instruction. I am going to have to challenge myself to get better at this. I am going to try and start small by including a formative assessment into every lesson. I am going to have to be more scientific in my approach. I am going to have to teach more like a scientist.

Teacher Journal

I have been sitting in this bookstore for hours looking through different books on teaching trying to get ideas to take back with me into my classroom. There are a ton of books on the subject of education in here. There are so many ways you can teach, how do you decide? What kind of teacher do you want to be? What kind of teacher are you going to be? I stare at the words on the page of the current book I'm browsing and begin to reflect on my own practice? I ask myself, what kind of teacher am I going to be? I sit back in the big plush chair and try to come up with an answer. I am going to be a great teacher. I am going to push myself to be the best teacher I can be. I'm going to teach like I want to be teacher of the year. How else would anybody want to teach?, but like that of a teacher who wants to win a teacher of the year award. I am going to find someone who has won this award and imitate them. I am going to find as many people as I can who have won this award and ask them for their best teaching secrets. Maybe, I can write a book on best teaching strategies one day. I am going to teach like I want to be teacher of the year.

Teacher Journal

Do not judge yourself by your successes but judge yourself by your failures. I'm not sure where I first heard that saying or why it popped into my head at that exact moment, but I immediately thought about some of my failures in the classroom. I thought about the Melvins', the Ceasers' and the long list of kids that I had probably let down over the years. I am going to have to do better. I am going to have to dig deep to turn my failures into success. I am going to have to do more than be teacher of the year. I am going to have to teach like I want them to put my statue outside the school. Yes, I am going to teach like I want my statue outside the school.

I start to think back to when I first got into education. I remember working as a teacher's assistant in college and thinking how great of a teacher I wanted to be. I remember thinking I would never be an average teacher. I remember how motivated and excited I was when I was accepted into the Teach for America program. I am going to be that great teacher I wanted to be. I am going to teach with passion and fire. I am going to teach like I want them to put my name on the building. Teach like you want them to put your name on the building.

Teacher Journal

Family Engagement! What am I going to do about family engagement and parental involvement? I have just finished taking a teacher self-evaluation and this is the only area where I gave myself a 1 (ineffective)score. I think back to our parent teacher night, when no parents showed up, and I think to myself, I have to do better in this specific area. My new goal is to score as many 4's (highly effective) as possible on the state teacher practice standards. I look back at the family engagement section again. The rubric says that a highly effective teacher will deliberately, purposefully and regularly use tools to help foster parent communication and be thoughtful about language, transportation and technological needs. What am I going to do to improve my parent engagement?

****

I keep thinking about this family engagement problem. I am going to create a parent survey and collect parent contact information so that I can contact parents more often. I am going to create a google classroom and leave a weekly message so parents can keep track of what's going on. I am going to the next training offered by my school to find out about our automated messaging system for student's families. I am going to

conduct a home visit so that I can really earn a 4 (highly effective) on my
next self-evaluation.

****

Today is the day! I can't believe I'm actually going to do this. I am going to conduct my first home visits ever. Why am I so nervous? I looked up a ton of articles on how to prepare for a home visit on the web. I got a lot of helpful tips from various education sites. Start with the positive, be prepared, remember the important points and practice good manners were just some of the helpful tips that I had written down. But who should I go see first? I put the names of my most challenging students from each of my six classes in a baseball cap and pull out a name. I unfold the piece of paper and read the name. Caeser!

Teacher Journal

I felt uncomfortable driving through the maze of streets in the Nickerson Garden Projects. It takes very little time to identify the signs of poverty and to understand how strong the gang culture is in this neighborhood. I see red chucks, red hoodies and red bandanas almost everywhere I look, but I just keep reminding myself this is where I am needed. I try to convince myself that I am welcome here, but I can't help but feel like an outsider or some type of intruder trespassing into this neighborhood.

I really didn't know what to expect as I pulled up to Caesars home. What am I doing here? I should have called first. Should I have brought someone with me? Maybe, I should just leave. What if you knock on the wrong door? What if someone thinks I'm a cop? Why am I wearing blue Converse sneakers? The doubt was back, and it was quickly intensifying into fear. Calm down, calm down, relax, I keep saying to myself. I am only here to meet with families and to help kids. If you want to be a great teacher this is what it's going to take.

I open the car door and begin to quickly walk through a cluster of homes along a pathway up to Casers door. I timidly knock on the door secretly hoping no one would answer. I will myself to knock again harder this time and I hear someone approaching the door. Caesar opens the door, and just stares at me with a mix of amazement, confusion, and horror on his face.

What's up sir? I say, trying to play it cool and not feel awkward. Caesar just nods his head and continues to stare, I guess he's still trying to process what I'm doing here. An older lady comes up behind Caesar speaking in Spanish trying to see who is at the door. She says a few words to Caesar and from my limited Spanish, I can tell he replies it's his bad teacher. The lady gives me a grave look but motions for me to come in.

Buenos dias senora. I say feeling quite proud of myself. Mi nombre es Mr. Shaw. Yo soy maestro de tu nino Caesar. Yo quiero presentarme y conocer a la familia. I say to the lady now feeling less confident. Caesar looks at me as if I'm crazy. The lady looks very confused at my attempt at speaking Spanish but gives a big laugh and says muy bien, senior, gracias. She offers for me to sit down on the couch and we begin to talk.

The next hour and a half was extremely eye opening and had a huge impact on me. I learned so much about Caesar and his family during this home visit. I have always worked in rough areas, so I was used to working with kids whose families might have been struggling financially or had tough situations but this visit really helped me to understand how much these things can impact students. I always had a no excuses mentality in the classroom, but this visit helped to shift my thinking and change my perspective.

Caesar was living with his grandmother in a one - bedroom unit with his two little sisters ages three and five. I learned that his mother had been deported back to Mexico nearly a year ago. His grandmother informed me that her son Caesar's dad was in prison and was not due for release for several years. She told me that they were living on government assistance and that she lately often times feels very ill. She is worried about what will happen with the children if something happens to her. She tells me their mom wants them to stay here in America to have a better life. She told me she has not spoken to anyone at the school or asked anyone for any kind of help because she does not know who she can trust.

Theresa, Caesar's grandmother only speaks Spanish so of course Caesar had to translate all of this. She told me about how the gangs were relentlessly pursuing Caesar and pressuring him to join their gang or else. She spoke of how desperate they were for money and were struggling to get by. She told me about the bugs and mice that plagued their apartment even though she cleans day and night. She explained how hard it was to get enough food and how the food bank and the church were essential to their survival. The more Theresa spoke about their circumstances the more anxious, tense and aggravated Caesar seemed to get. He was breaking down and beginning to cry. I saw the frustration and sadness in Caesar, and it was just all too clear. It was a perfect reminder why we can't teach kids until their most basic needs are met.

Caesar walks out on to the porch holding his shirt over his face. I walked out there with him and not knowing exactly what to say I put my arm around him and say everything is going to be o.k.. We are going to figure something out I say. He put his face into my chest and begin to sob. Why? Why is this happening to me? Why did they leave me here? Why don't they love me, he asks between sobs? I am speechless. I pat him on the back trying to console him while struggling to hold back my own tears. His grandmother walks out onto the porch holding his youngest sister in one arm and puts her other hand on his shoulder to show her support for him.

We all stand here on the porch in silence for a few moments. Hey Caesar, I say wiping the tears from my eyes. I owe you an apology. I'm sorry for how I've treated you. I was wrong and I'm going to be a better teacher from now on. I extend out my hand and he slowly reaches for it. I pull him in an give him a big hug. Everything is going to be o.k. I promise you. we are going to get your family all the help we can. Caesar looks up with his big brown eyes and smiles and says cool, I mean thanks, I appreciate that. We really need help! I will see you back in class on Monday right? Yea, I will be there, but I don't have a backpack or anything like that. Don't worry about that. I will take care of all that, just make sure you're in class.

I say goodbye to Caesar, his sisters and his grandmother. I'm walking to my car trying to process everything that just happened. Once I'm in the car, I reflect on some of the difficult realities some of my students must face. I think about Caesar and his situation. What is the best way to attack these issues? What is the best support we can give them? What are the best remedies for students attending schools and growing up in emergency areas of need?

Discussion Questions

1. What are you going to do to be different in the classroom?

2. What is your mantra/class motto going to be?

3. What kind of teacher do you want to be?

4. How are you going to promote family engagement?

5. What can you do for the Caesar in your classroom?

Chapter Eight

A call to Action

Alert! Alert! Alert!

This is not a drill.

Alert! Alert! Alert! This is a code blue emergency.

This is a code blue emergency. Alert! Alert! Alert! This is not a drill. All stakeholders please respond to your assigned areas immediately! This is a code blue emergency!

That is what you are most likely to hear in a hospital during an emergency when a patient is in grave danger. This is also what we should hear playing over the intercom in our elementary and secondary schools across the nation every day. Educators, this is not a drill, this an educational emergency. This is a code blue situation. There is no time to waste. We must respond with urgency and purpose. Students growing up and attending schools in distressed urban areas need your immediate help. We can no longer sit back and continue our practice as normal. We must answer the call before it is too late.

Throughout this book, we have explored the state of education in the urban community. We have identified the tremendous challenges that urban schools, teachers, students and families must face on a daily basis. We have reviewed how to observe, diagnose, prescribe and treat student's academic, mental, physical, social and spiritual needs. We have discussed possible remedies and prescriptions for the most common issues in the classroom. We have also discussed new ideas, practices and strategies to implement in the urban classroom. Now, that you have decided to answer the call, what will you do next? How will you decide to adjust your practice to implement emergency teaching? What activities and strategies will you utilize in your classroom? In this last chapter, we will look at some of my favorite ways to implement these ideas in the classroom.

Teach with Character Traits

1. Character Characters

In this activity, students are given a slip of paper with a negative or positive character trait written down on it. Students are expected to get into character and display the actions of a person with the character trait they received on their piece of paper. During the last few minutes of class students are allowed to try and guess each other's primary character trait based on the student's attitude, actions and behavior in class that day. We then have a small discussion about the importance of positive character traits at the end of the activity.

Teach with Community

2. KUDOS

A Kudos activity is a great and simple way to build community in the classroom. Kudos awards are a fun activity we do in our classroom every Friday. Students are allowed to fill out kudos certificates for their classmates throughout the week. Students are allowed to present the award in front of the class to their classmates at the end of the week. Students award kudos to each other for being kind, helpful or even being a good friend. This is a fun community building activity that also helps to strengthen students speaking and presentation skills as well.

Teach with Courage

3. Home Visit

It takes a lot of courage to be an educator. There are always going to be moments when you must stand up for yourself and your students. One activity that requires a great deal of courage is conducting a home visit. Conducting home visits can be a powerful experience for urban teachers. There are tremendous benefits to conducting homes visits such as building relationships, building trust, showing extra effort, breaking down barriers, soliciting parent volunteers and community building. Most importantly, conducting home visits shows your level of dedication to your students and their families. A teacher conducting home visits is a teacher teaching with courage.

Teach with Discipline

#4. The Rollout

Obviously, there are many aspects to consider when discussing discipline in the classroom. Teachers must consider rules, consequences, positive reinforcement, referrals and progressive discipline among many other things. But, one of the most important elements when establishing rules, regulations and procedures in the classroom is the rollout. The rollout is the introduction to a new rule or procedure in the classroom. In this activity the teacher explains that a new rule or procedure is being established. Secondly, the teacher explains why this rule was necessary to implement in the classroom. The teacher then models or describes what this should look like in the classroom. Lastly, the students practice, or role play this new rule in various scenarios.

Teach with empathy

#5 Viewpoint Activity

One of my favorite lessons for teaching empathy is the viewpoint activity. During this lesson students work in small groups of about three to four students. Students are all given the same scenario to read but each group is assigned a specific character in the scenario to focus on. After a few minutes of reading and note taking, the groups begin to discuss the scenario from their characters viewpoint. Students begin to build empathy by listening to each other and trying to understand and relate to others as opposed to arguing or trying to persuade the other groups to see things their way.

Teach with enthusiasm

#6 Nick Names and Secret Handshakes

Teaching with enthusiasm means showing excitement and loving what you do. I love to show my devotion by greeting my students at the door. I confirm to my students that I am excited to see them and start the day by doing this nicknames and handshakes activity each day. As students come through the door, I go through a unique secret handshake that I have made with each student. Some students don't prefer the handshake experience, so I call them by a particular nickname (approved by them, of course). This activity helps me to build unique relationships and shows the kids that I am pumped up and excited about the day of learning ahead.

Teach with a Growth Mindset

#7 Not Yet Activity

Developing a growth mindset is one of the most important things you can do in an urban classroom. In this activity, students are all given a coloring worksheet with the word YET on it. Students color in the word YET and began to fill out things around the worksheet that students cannot do well yet, in their classes. A child who is struggling in math might put down subtracting fractions or solving one step equations. We then place these worksheets inside the cover of student's binders. As students' progress throughout the year, they can go through and cross things off the worksheet that they improved upon. This activity promotes the idea of a growth mindset.

Teach with High Expectations

#8 Consistency is the key

Holding high expectations is absolutely critical for all teachers working in emergency areas of need. I have learned that holding high expectations for students really means holding high expectations for myself. If I ask for headings to be written in pen that means not giving in and just letting one-person slide. Holding high expectations means setting your criteria before the school year begins and being consistent and sticking to it.

Teach with Hope & Faith

#9 Daily Affirmations

Hope and faith can be powerful tools in urban education. I use daily affirmations as a way to infuse the ideas of hope and faith into my classroom. I make sure to start each class session with a daily affirmation. The goal of the daily affirmation is to build student's self - confidence and faith in themselves. My goal is to help students build a positive and optimistic mindset. I want students to build up an unbreakable confidence in themselves and their ability to succeed. I also want students to be optimistic and expect positive things to happen in their lives in and out of the classroom.

Teach with Love

#10 Five Minute Birthday Party

Love is the greatest teaching strategy that any teacher can utilize. There are an infinite number of ways to show love every day in the classroom. I correlate love in the classroom with acts of compassion, affection, generosity and kindness toward each other. I encourage love in the classroom by asking my kids to be polite to each other and practice proper manners. My favorite activity for displaying love in the classroom is celebrating birthdays. We make sure to acknowledge the birthday of every student in my class. We even make sure to acknowledge the summer birthdays. We have a five-minute party each month to celebrate these special days. We decorate the classroom; students bring balloons and we listen to music and dance. This is my favorite activity for teaching with love.

Teach with Magic

#11 One Minute Dance Party

Every urban teacher must incorporate a little bit of magic into their lessons. The one-minute dance party is a great way to incorporate magic into your classroom. At the beginning of the year, I have students complete a music interest survey. I use the songs from these assessments to play during our one minute dance parties. I enjoy this activity because it allows me to incorporate music and dance into the classroom in a fun and creative way. The one-minute dance party is a great way to bring magic into the classroom.

Teach with Purpose

#12 Share your message

Teachers working in emergency areas of need must teach with purpose. My purpose is clear. My purpose is to close the achievement gap, help students become college or career ready, and help my students become the best people they can be. I aim to achieve this goal by being strategic and purposeful in my lesson planning, pacing and instruction. I also make sure to constantly share this purpose with my students. Each year, I give students a welcome letter that I require them to keep readily available for the entire year. In this letter, I tell students what my goals are, what our purpose is and why education is so important. Being an emergency teacher means teaching with purpose.

Teach with Resilience

#13 Introduce them to failure

Resiliency is one trait that I want to foster in all my students. Resiliency is the ability to bounce back and recover from challenging, frustrating or difficult situations. I try to help my students experience failure as quickly as possible in my classroom. I love to challenge my students and present them with fun challenging materials such as complex word searches, mazes, riddles, group challenges and various other academic materials. My objective is to teach students not to give up and to try and work through difficult problems. I want students to learn that they may fail at something but that is not an invitation to quit but an opportunity to try again. Additionally, I want students to know that sometimes they will have to continue to work to develop some skills or accomplish more complicated task.

Teach with Rigor

#14 Academic Vocabulary

There are many instructional strategies that a teacher can use to help make lessons more rigorous. One strategy that I often utilize is the use of academic vocabulary. I require my students to use key academic words as often as possible during class discussions. I also randomly call on students to define or describe key words posted on the word wall. Getting students to use appropriate academic vocabulary helps to increase the level of rigor of a lesson.

Teach with Role Models

#15 Guest Speakers

The power of a positive influence is immeasurable. Students growing up in disadvantaged urban areas can never be exposed to enough positive role models. I try to introduce my students to positive role models in addition to positive character traits as often as possible. One of my favorite activities for bringing positive role models into the classroom is inviting guest speakers out to present. It can be very challenging to find guest speakers, but it is definitely worth the time and effort.

Teach with urgency

#16 Close the Achievement Gap

There is always time to smile or to laugh but there is no time to waste. Teachers working in disadvantaged emergency areas must teach with a sense of urgency. We are on a mission to close the achievement gap and to get kids caught up, proficient and college ready. I try to reinforce this idea with my students every day. I always take time to celebrate small milestones but then I am pushing my kids toward the next goal. I tell my students there is no time to rest in a race until we catch up and then it is time to work even harder.

Teacher Journal

I am so excited for the start of the second semester. The events that have transpired over the past three weeks have changed me forever. I am more motivated and determined than ever to teach our urban youth. My purpose and passion for teaching have been renewed. I am going to focus on turning my weaknesses into strengths and my failures into successes. I have developed a new positive mindset and positive attitude and have realized that good teaching goes far beyond the walls of the classroom.

These experiences have also taught me that I must whole heartedly believe in my students and their gifts and abilities. I learned that I must not only hold high expectations for my students but for myself as well. I must come to the classroom each day prepared and ready to change lives. I must accept only the very best effort and not let anything go unnoticed or let any student slide by. I must use every student behavioral misstep as a learning opportunity and not as a moment to punish. I must hold each student accountable and demand maximum effort from each student.

I learned that I must develop creative, rigorous and engaging lessons. I learned that the curriculum should be culturally relevant and interesting to my student population. I learned that I must teach students to develop a growth mindset. I learned that I must be seriously consistent on my rewards and progressive discipline system. I learned that I need to be enthusiastic about learning and make lessons fun. I learned that it is vital to teach with a sense of urgency. I learned that it is necessary to teach with empathy and to teach students about empathy. I learned that I must teach students to be hopeful and to have faith. I learned that it is crucial that students be exposed to mentors and role models. I learned that I must build strong relationships with my students. I learned that it is of severe importance that we teach students to be courageous and resilient. I learned that we must teach students about positive character traits and good citizenship. I learned that we must teach with love and teach our students to love each other and most importantly, Love themselves.

Discussion questions

1. Do you teach with a sense of urgency?

2. How can we incorporate more rigor into our lessons?

3. What is your purpose in the classroom?

4. Explain one way you can teach with magic?

5. What is one way you will teach with love?

Chapter Nine

Eleven Recommendations for Improving Education in Urban Schools

A Note to Education Leaders:

Based on my experiences as an urban classroom teacher, I've identified eleven key recommendations for improving the urban teaching and learning experience. If you are a teacher in an urban area serving a high concentration of minority students in high-needs areas, share this list (and this book) with your administrators and school board members to adopt and bolster academic success. If you are an education leader, I encourage you to implement these ideas to support the students and educators in your school or district.

Hire Exceptional Teachers

The most critical factor in student achievement is teacher effectiveness. Minority students attending schools in urban low-income neighborhoods are in crucial need of exceptional teachers. Unfortunately, schools in emergency areas tend to have a higher rate of teacher turnover and a lower average of years of teaching experience than most suburban schools. These two factors often contribute to issues of student discipline and poor student achievement in urban schools.

An exceptional teacher is one who uses a variety of instructional strategies fluidly and moves from one strategy to another as the student and the curriculum requires. Additionally, these teachers effectively plan lessons and differentiate instruction based on the individual needs of the student. An exceptional teacher consistently uses effective strategies and procedures to address issues of student discipline and classroom management. They embrace cooperative learning and provide opportunities for students to discuss and work collaboratively. These teachers provide rigorous, culturally relevant lessons through a combination of varied learning modalities and domains of learning activities. Exceptional teachers strongly encourage parental support and seek to inform students and parents of valuable community resources available to students and their families. These teachers hold high expectations for all students and are great at challenging, motivating, and inspiring their students to strive for excellence in and out of the classroom.

Exceptional teachers reflect on their own perspectives and are aware of how their own hidden biases may affect their classroom leadership. They continuously work to develop empathy and understanding of the students they serve, inform their students about important societal issues that affect their community, and use every opportunity to incorporate these issues into the lesson and curriculum. Most importantly, exceptional teachers create strong relationships with their students.

Reduce Class Size

There is not a substantial amount of research that suggests class size has a significant impact on student academic achievement, but it has been generally accepted that as a class size decreases, the allotment of time that a teacher can spend with each student increases. This increased amount of time that a teacher can spend with each student is precious and vital to improving academic achievement. If a student/teacher ratio cannot be lowered due to do budget restraints, finding solutions to increase interaction time between teachers and low performing students would be a good idea.

Hire Veteran Teachers

It has been well established through research literature that teacher experience has a significant positive effect on student achievement. Data suggests that there is a positive correlation between experienced teachers and higher standardized test scores. In addition to raising achievement veteran teachers are very impactful at positively affecting the culture of a campus. Additionally, veteran teachers may bring several tools and strategies to the table that could help improve instruction and behavior on the campus overall.

Extend the School Year

There is an educational achievement gap in the United States. If minority students are going to catch up and close the gap, it might be necessary for these students to go to school more than their counterparts. Schools serving students in disadvantaged neighborhoods should look to reduce summer break and extend the school year. This longer year could be an incentive to motivate students to perform as well. Students who do not succeed on the appropriate benchmarks could be required to continue to attend school. Students could use this additional time to continue to master objectives and the reduction of student population during the summer will allow for more time for teachers to spend with the remaining individual students. Just like the majority of hospitals that offer emergency care, the schools in emergency areas of need should always be open and ready to serve.

(Cont.) Extend the School Hours

Six hours per day and about one-hundred-and-eighty days makes up the average school year. This has not been enough time for a significant portion of at-risk students to demonstrate proficiency on their specific grade-level standards and objectives. If a student requires two to three times longer to master math standards or objectives as the average student, won't that student require more time than the average student to become proficient? Schools serving minority students in low-income neighborhoods should look to extend school operating hours. A parent should be able to bring their child in at 7:00 p.m. and get help with homework from an experienced certified teacher. Students that are highly motivated to excel or catch up should be provided the opportunity to take classes in the evening as well. Just like most hospitals that offer emergency care, the schools in emergency areas of need should always be open and ready to treat individual's needs.

Use Effective Strategies and Best Practices School-wide

Despite the critics, there are some great teachers, great teaching and amazing practices taking place in urban schools. What is not happening nearly often enough is the sharing and execution of these best practices and procedures on a school wide level. Schools should establish the best behavioral, intervention, and instructional strategies and procedures and encourage the use of these strategies across a content, grade or school wide level. Students would benefit tremendously from the uniformity of these practices being utilized school wide. In addition to the students, the overall school culture could improve through the use of consistent implementation and enforcement of best practices school wide.

Provide Strategic Intervention for the 33%

Based on my observations as a teacher, it appears that nearly a third of all students in urban classrooms are struggling to master subject specific standards, especially in subjects like math and science. All schools should have strategic intervention plans in place to address the "thirty-three" percent of students that are struggling with basic skills or struggling to keep up with the curriculum. Schools serving in disadvantaged areas must identify these students and create a solid plan to provide intervention to those students that are not yet proficient.

Incorporate Social Justice/Service Learning

Schools located in emergency areas should strongly consider integrating social justice or service learning into the curriculum of the school. Social justice education can be described as an educational approach that draws connections between curriculum and current day real world social and political issues. A benefit of social justice education is that it requires students to reflect on the world and how social justice issues might affect them and their community. Social justice education gives students the tools to become positive agents of change in their community. The goal of social justice education is to get students to reflect and understand how academic achievement can help them be better prepared to create change on a global scale.

Service learning has been described as an educational approach that blends traditional instruction with the opportunity to volunteer and serve in the community. Service learning gives students the opportunity to see the curriculum come to life in real world settings. The benefit of service learning is that it allows students to develop critical thinking and problem-solving skills in real world situations. Additionally, it gives students an opportunity to interact with diverse populations and exposes them to new environments and situations.

Create a Positive Culture

Creating a positive climate is critical for schools located in disadvantaged neighborhoods. Students who continually face an excessive amount of trauma and stress are far more likely to shut down or become resistant if they began to face discouragement at school. Administrators, teachers and staff must make a determined effort to make every single interaction, with students who face risk, as positive as possible. Urban teachers must be sure to provide positive feedback and supportive encouragement. Students should feel supported, confident and uplifted from the very first day they step on campus until well after they have graduated. A positive interaction could make all the difference on a bad day.

Consider the Avid Effect

The power of AVID cannot be denied! Avid is an acronym which stands for Advancement Via Individual Determination. The Avid system is a non-profit academic program which uses researched based strategies, activities and curriculum to help develop student's social and academic skills. Rigor, relevance and relationships are at the heart of the Avid program. Avid's philosophy is that if you hold students to the highest standards and provide the proper amount of academic and social support, students will rise to meet the challenge.

Avid provides this necessary support by teaching and developing the skills and behaviors necessary for college and career success. Avid uses the WICOR model as the highly engaging structure for providing academic support. The WICOR model calls for a focus in the areas of Writing, Inquiry, Collaboration, Organization and Reading. Teachers use the WICOR model to help guide students through rigorous, relevant, and inquiry-based lessons.

Avid not only helps create better students, Avid helps to create better teachers as well. Avid believes that when teachers are deeply engaged students will become engaged. Avid provides support for teachers by providing a tremendous amount of resources such as materials and weekly lesson plans. Additionally, Avid host numerous professional developments and summer institutes throughout the nation.

The mission of the Avid program is to close the achievement gap by preparing all students, especially those that are traditionally underrepresented in higher education, for college readiness and success in a global society. Every school, working with students who may be struggling to stay on the path to college or career readiness should consider incorporating AVID into their program.

Get & Keep the Family Involved

Academic research seems to support the idea that there are many benefits to positive parental support and involvement in the student learning process. Research suggests that parental and family involvement helps to not only benefit students but helps to improve the schooling process for the teacher, the school and the parents alike. Every urban school, especially those located in high crime or economically distressed neighborhoods must consider strategies to get parents positively involved within the school and engaged in their students learning experience. Research reports indicate that regardless of race or social economic status, students that have positive parental or family support tend to achieve more, get better grades and come to school more regularly than their peers that do not have such support. Furthermore, students with positive parental or family support also report higher levels of self-esteem and motivation. Parental and family support provides almost as many benefits for teachers, schools and parents as they do for students. Parents may benefit by gaining an increased understanding of their student's curriculum, develop better relationships with their student's teachers, and parents might gain a better understanding of the goals and duties of the school. Teachers might benefit by improving the overall communication between themselves and the parents. Schools might benefit by improving its reputation and experiencing greater community support. There is little doubt that getting positive parental or family support can be a challenge due to a number of obvious reasons, but it is still an important challenge that every school must address.

Professional Learning Communities

We have all heard the old African Proverb – It takes a village to raise a child. This is as true today as it was a thousand years ago. After reading through hundreds of academic journals and reflecting on my own practice, it has become evident to me that quite possibly one of the single most powerful things we can do as an educational community is develop powerful, purposeful and meaningful professional learning communities. Research literature makes it abundantly clear that professional learning communities done correctly have tremendous benefits for both the student and the teacher [14] The benefits of Professional developments are well known. Teachers are able to work collaboratively instead of in isolation. Teachers are given a chance to be renewed and reenergized. Teachers are introduced to new concepts and strategies. Teachers are able to learn and share best practices. Students of teachers who are routinely deeply engaged in Professional learning communities generally report higher standardized scores, lower absenteeism, greater gains and are less likely to drop out of school. We all know the benefits of Professional Learning communities done correctly. Unfortunately, too many schools located in emergency areas of need are not fully invested in the PLC. The PLC should be constant and recurring cycles of action research focused on classroom rigor, academic instruction or classroom management. The PLC should be a collaborative process where the teachers have a voice and bring their most pressing issues to the forefront for discussion and study. Any school that is serious about changing the academic culture in an economically at-risk urban neighborhood must be seriously committed to creating a true Professional learning community.

[14]Wilson, A. (2016). From Professional Practice to Practical Leader: Teacher Leadership in Professional Learning Communities. International Journal of Teacher Leadership, 7(2), 45–62.

About the Author

West Shaw is a social justice educator, dedicated to closing the achievement gap and improving the state of urban education in the United States. Mr. Shaw is currently a seventh-grade Avid – Leadership teacher in Las Vegas, Nevada. West Shaw began his career in education as a teacher's assistant for Long Beach Unified School District in California. Mr. Shaw graduated from California State University, Long Beach with a degree in Sociology. He earned a master's degree in education from California State University, Dominguez Hills with an emphasis in curriculum and instruction. Shaw earned a second Master's degree in education from U.C.L.A., with an emphasis in urban teaching. Later achieving a third Masters and administrative credential from National University. West Shaw was later accepted into the "Teach for America" program, where he served in his hometown of Los Angeles, California. Mr. Shaw is currently pursuing his doctoral degree in K-12 education with an emphasis in organizational leadership. His career aspirations are to be dean of students at the middle school level and to teach adjunct educational courses at the college level. Shaw's dream is to open an academy that promotes a culture of academic excellence, cultural awareness, character development, and leadership for urban and minority youth built on the principles of Black and Latino Greek-letter organizations. West Shaw is a proud member of Phi Beta Sigma Fraternity Incorporated and strongly believes in their motto, "Culture for service and service for humanity."

Acknowledgements

I have been truly inspired by the work of Dr. Tolu Noah, Dr. Victor Rios, Dr. Shaun Woodly, Dr. V.C. Jones and Dr. Eduardo Lopez. Thank you for all the work you do for our students and community. Thank you for being an inspiration.

I would like to give a huge shout out to Principal Amen Rahh. Thank you for laying the blueprint and showing us how to build an amazing school in an emergency area of need. The work that you are doing at University Pathway Public Service Academy is Incredible. Keep up the great work. Here comes the Boom!

I want to say thank you to **Empire Publishing** for helping to bring this project to life. A special thank you to Francesca for being so encouraging, patient and supportive.

Thank you to my wonderful Instagram teacher/friend @Mommyteacherfashionista for being a supportive voice every step of the way. Best of luck on the release of your new book!

I would like to thank Marisol R. for helping me to reflect on my perceptions and misconceptions of working in urban areas and educating minority youth. I am forever grateful.

A special thank you to my mother and brother for helping to bring me up and guide me in the right direction. Thank you from the bottom of my heart.

Amanni, thank you for all your love and support. I am so proud of you. I am excited to see how far you will go in life. Keep up the great work. Hard work – Pays off!

Jazmine, thank you for your kindness, patience, love and support. Thank you for believing in me, supporting me and encouraging me to achieve my goals. Thank you for continually pushing me to step out of my comfort zone and try new things. I love you now and forever.

Interested in contacting West Shaw for a speaking engagement or other educational events please contact him:

Website: WWW.ITEACHURBAN.COM

Instagram: ITEACHURBAN

Email: 1WESTSHAW@GMAIL.COM

Facebook: West Shaw

Twitter: ITEACHURBAN

References

Aguilar, D. N. (2014). Oppression, Domination, Prison: The Mass Incarceration of Latino and African American Men. Vermont Connection, 35, 12–20.

Alderman, M. k. (2008). Motivation for Achievement. (Third edition). New York: Routledge.

Bandura, A. (1986). Social Foundations of thought and action: A social Cognitive theory. New Jersey: Prentice - Hall.

Blue, L. (2012). Motivation, not IQ, matters most for learning new math skills. Retrieved from http://www.healthland.time.com.

Boykin, A. W., & Noguera, P. (2011). Creating the opportunity to learn: Moving from research to practice to close the achievement gap. Alexandria, Virginia: Association for supervision and curriculum development.

Carroll, T. (2009). The Next Generation of Learning Teams. Phi Delta Kapplan 91(1), 38-43.

DePaoli, J. L., Fox, J. H., Ingram, E. S., Maushard, M., Bridgeland, J. M., Balfanz, R., ... Alliance for Excellent Education. (2015). Building a Grad Nation: Progress and Challenge in Ending the High School Dropout Epidemic. Annual Update 2015. Civic Enterprises.

Dweck, C. S. (2006). Mindset: The new psychology of success. New York, NY: Random House.

Felitti, V. et al. (1998). Relationship of Childhood Abuse and Household Dysfunction to many of the Leading causes of Death in

Adults. American Journal of Preventive Medicine Volume 14, pages 245 – 258.

Freire, P. (1982). Pedagogy of the oppressed New York, New York: Continuum.

Fuller, B., Waite, A., & Torres Irribarra, D. (2016). Explaining Teacher Turnover: School Cohesion and Intrinsic Motivation in Los Angeles. American Journal of Education, 122(4), 537–567.

Gaines, G. F., & Southern Regional Education Board, A. G. (2001). Focus on Teacher Salaries: An Update on Average Salaries and Recent Legislative Actions in the SREB States.

Gamble, B. E., & Lambros, K. M. (2014). Provider Perspectives on School-Based Mental Health for Urban Minority Youth: Access and Services. Journal of Urban Learning, Teaching, and Research, 10, 25–38.

Hoerr, T.R. (2017). The formative five: Fostering grit, empathy, and other successful skills every student needs. Alexandria, Virginia: ASCD.

Jackson, C. K., Johnson, R. C., & Persico, C. (2015). Boosting Educational Attainment and Adult Earnings: Does School Spending Matter after All? Education Next, 15(4), 69–76.

Lemov, D. (2010). Teach like a champion: Forty-Nine Techniques that put students on the path to college. San Francisco, Ca: Jossey-Bass.

Norman, J. (2015). Young, Poor, Urban Dwellers Most Likely to Be Crime Victims. Social and Policy Issuses 32(1) 12-15.

Silver, D. (2012). Fall down 7 times, get up 8: Teaching kids to succeed. Thousand Oaks, Ca: Corwin.

Price, J. H., Khubchandani, J., McKinney, M., & Braun, R. (2013). Racial/ethnic disparities in chronic diseases of youths and access to health care in the United States. BioMed Research International.

Toldson, I. A. (2011). Editor's Comment: How Black Boys with Disabilities End Up in Honors Classes While Others without Disabilities End Up in Special Education. Journal of Negro Education, 80(4), 439–444.

Tough, P. (2012). How children succeed. Grit, curiosity, and the hidden power of character. Boston, MA: Huffington Mifflin Harcourt.

Veiga Rodrigues, C., Figueiredo, A. B., Rocha, S., Ward, S., & Braga Tavares, H. (2018). Risky Behaviors on a Student's Population. Journal of Alcohol & Drug Education, 62(1), 46–70.

Wagner, T. (2008). The Global Achievement Gap: Why even our best schools don't teach the new survival skills our children need - and what we can do about it. New York, New York: Basic Books.

Weber, K. (2010). Waiting for "Superman": how we can save Americas failing public schools. New York: Public Affairs.